"Here is the rare book that anticipates with commonsense intelligence the most practical problems of how we will inhabit our landscape in the 21st century. The author recognizes the macro trends of downscaling and re-localization that will determine how we live in a coming period of industrial de-growth, changing climate, and social crisis. The writing is straightforward, clear, and muscular, conveying an urgent and purposeful spirit of facing the facts and getting things done."

— **James Howard Kunstler,** Author of *The Geography of Nowhere, The Long Emergency,* and *World Made by Hand*

"In this ground-breaking book, Korkut Onaran tackles the inconvenient truth that humans must adapt to the accelerating impacts of climate change: where we'll live, how we'll live – and how we can successfully live together. This is an indispensable starting point for charting a resilient and humane future."

—**Rick Cole,** Executive Director of The Congress for the New Urbanism (CNU)

Urbanism for a Difficult Future

Urbanism for a Difficult Future: Practical Responses to the Climate Crisis is a much-needed guide to launching the next generation of land use planning and urbanism that will enable us to adapt to and survive the consequences of climate change.

The book offers strong, straightforward measures for creating a landscape of resilience via pockets of self-sufficiencies. It demonstrates how to secure systems that sustain life (energy, water, food, waste, and production of essential goods) as well as political and social protocols enabling agile decision-making in managing these systems effectively at local levels. It also provides the design principles for creating a built environment that will enable the kind of localization we need for adaptation. The book explores how it is possible to create a life that does not depend on large-scale regional sustenance systems which are likely to be disrupted or fail.

This book uncovers how to enable people to be creative, productive, and supportive at local levels, so that we can achieve strong and diverse local economies that can sustain life. It will appeal to students, planners, and policy makers working in environmental studies, environmental engineering, urban and regional planning, architecture, landscape architecture, and urbanism.

Korkut Onaran is a founder principal of Pel-Ona Architects and Urbanists. He also teaches as adjunct in the College of Architecture and Planning, University of Colorado Denver. Urbanism, regulation cultures, and development codes have been a focus of his teaching and practice. His book

Crafting Form-based Codes: Resilient Design, Policy, and Regulation was published by Routledge in 2019.

Andrés Duany is one of the founders and intellectual fathers of the international New Urbanism movement. His sharp vision and inspiring talks have convinced many elected officials and professionals to encourage implementation of successful urbanism. He is also one of the founders of the Congress for the New Urbanism. As an architect, urban designer, planner, and author, he has produced plans for hundreds of new and renewed communities around the globe. He is the author of many essays and articles and co-author of several books including, *Suburban Nation: The Rise of Sprawl and the Decline of the American Dream*, *The Smart Code*, *The Smart Growth Manual*, *Garden Cities: Agricultural Urbanism*, and *The New Civic Art.*

Paul Crabtree is a visionary urbanist and civil engineer. He is the founder of Crabtree Group, Inc. (CGI). CGI projects have demonstrated that green infrastructure can outperform conventional infrastructure while reducing capital and operation costs. CGI was the Civil Engineer of Record for two projects (a residential neighborhood and a school), each which received the Colorado Sustainable Design Award for 2011. CGI is also the proud winner of three CNU Charter Awards (2010, 2018, and 2020). Paul's contribution to adaptation discussions has been essential.

Urbanism for a Difficult Future

Practical Responses to the
Climate Crisis

Korkut Onaran

**Foreword by
Andrés Duany**

**Afterword by
Paul Crabtree**

Routledge
Taylor & Francis Group

NEW YORK AND LONDON

Cover images: Upper right: a block at adaptation village (rendering by the author); Lower: a bird-eye view perspective of the village center at adaptation village (rendering by Ronnie Pelusio); Photographs from left to right: a courtyard gate, Cadiz, Spain (photograph by the author); Byzantian Cisterns, İstanbul, Turkey (Getty Images); a street view at Old Datça, Turkey (photograph by the author); a courtyard gate, Puerto Vallarta, Mexico (photograph by the author).

First published 2023
by Routledge
605 Third Avenue, New York, NY 10158

and by Routledge
4 Park Square, Milton Park, Abingdon, Oxon, OX14 4RN

Routledge is an imprint of the Taylor & Francis Group, an informa business

Library of Congress Cataloging-in-Publication Data
Names: Onaran, Korkut, author. | Duany, Andres, writer of foreword. | Crabtree, Paul (Civil eingineer), writer of afterword.
Title: Urbanism for a difficult future : practical responses to the climate crisis / Korkut Onaran ; foreword by Andrés Duany ; afterword by Paul Crabtree.
Description: New York, NY : Routledge, 2023. | Includes bibliographical references and index. |
Identifiers: LCCN 2022012861 (print) | LCCN 2022012862 (ebook) | ISBN 9781032022666 (hardback) | ISBN 9781032022659 (paperback) | ISBN 9781003182627 (ebook)
Subjects: LCSH: Urban ecology (Sociology) | Sustainable urban development.
Classification: LCC HT241 .O53 2023 (print) | LCC HT241 (ebook) | DDC 307.76—dc23/eng/20220321
LC record available at https://lccn.loc.gov/2022012861
LC ebook record available at https://lccn.loc.gov/2022012862

ISBN: 9781032022666 (hbk)
ISBN: 9781032022659 (pbk)
ISBN: 9781003182627 (ebk)

DOI: 10.4324/9781003182627

Typeset in Adobe Caslon Pro
by codeMantra

This book has been realized by the partial financial help of the Vinyl Siding Institute.

To Andrés Duany

CONTENTS

FOREWORD

This is an important book, not just because it is rare in its cohort, but in the tough stand it takes. First, because it is relentlessly prescient. It was delivered to the publishers at the very moment of the Glasgow Conference (November 2021). This event was a shock. It is a moment in history when every adult on Earth was in some way conscious of the crisis. And yet, the commitments made were not enough. Since then, therefore, the future it engages seems a distortion field. To most realists it was as if a great pall had permeated the mind – and yet, this book is optimistic! And it is not theoretical.

One must now know that holding global warming down to 2 degrees centigrade by reducing carbon emissions to 50 percent by 2030 and 100 percent by 2050 is impossible. The author confronts that our Earth will continue to warm for a century at least. Science confirms that the best-case scenario to *mitigate the causes* of climate change must be concurrent with the *adaptation to its impacts*.

Korkut Onaran and I have been discussing the ideas behind this book for years. We determined that whatever criticism we have encountered following their public presentation is a misunderstanding of time frames. The majority today focuses on the period 2030–2060, whereas this book envisions the period 2060–2090.

These 30-year tranches correspond to the social convention that defines generations: from being born to giving birth. By these tranches it is possible to put a human face on those who will be in charge and those who will be affected. By 2030 the Boomers will have finally checked out. By 2060 Gen X, which will have been most responsible for the mitigation, will be checking out. Millennials will be in charge until 2090, while Generation – Greta Thunberg's generation – will bear the full burden of the inevitable heat. It is for the Millennials that this book is written – or at least some of them, as within these generations there are subsets in the kinds of response to the climate catastrophe.

There are several sociodemographic segments that filter "the science." This number has grown to six that can already be identified. In the first are the "old denialists." They are waning in number but, in any case, they are obtuse beyond convincing, and so this book ignores them.

In the second segment are the "ethicists" – those who are dedicated to safeguarding all of nature, its creatures, and humanity, for love – or because it is "the right thing to do." Their epitome is the polar bear cub on a floating ice slab. Such ethicists, for historical reasons that cannot be covered here, are common in Northern Europe and rare in the United States. This book does not address them, as it makes no pretense of salvaging nature.

Then there are those who will do the right thing – but because it is fashionable. Unlike the ethicists, they are not prepared to actually suffer in pursuit of mitigation. They are subject to the insult of "greenwashing" or "virtue-signaling" by the ethicists. Yet they do care and love green so long as it is tasty, beautiful, and convenient. Their icons are many, including the Tesla, the organic avocado, and the surface of bamboo. They are called "cool greens." Designers love them!

In the fourth segment are the politicians whose favorite, easy argument is that mitigating climate change is good for business. From Clinton to Biden, the narrative is that the switch to renewable energy will create millions of jobs. Despite scandalous disappointments such as ethanol, everybody approves of these "greenbacks," which are accepted by the right. They are not necessarily as ethical or cool as the left.

The fifth segment, "the transitionalists," must not be confused with the "survivalists" of the cold war. Those were armed individuals ready to make a last stand against red hordes. Surviving climate change requires a community and control of the regional level to secure localized water, power, and food. Sometimes their activities are derided as "circling the wagons." But the best term is "transitionalists" – those who will have *adapted to the impacts* of climate change with carbon *mitigation* as a secondary consequence. As such, they are very different from the former three. It is primarily to this segment that this book is addressed. They will understand what is being proposed, while the other segments won't.

Then, to these must be added one last: the emerging "party-on" segment. They would seem to be denialists, but are far from it. They are perhaps the most realistic of all. They have concluded from the evidence that mitigation is futile and the most rational response is to enjoy whatever days remain. They are great company, and we have nothing to offer them that Margaritaville does not already do.

And so, the reader has been introduced: this book will not make as much sense if you are inherently, by nature, among five of the sociodemographic segments described – yet there is overlap. This book does have some appeal to the business people of the fourth segment, as the communities to be built will involve entrepreneurs working for money. Good old American business will resonate, as usual, with what needs to be done.

And … if the design of these communities is truly well done, the Greens too will flock in – with the latest food, clothing, and rides. The truly disappointed will be the ethicists. They will be bothered by the futility of the Glasgow attempt being called out. They will be affronted by what will seem to them to be lack of ambition.

The program leading to Glasgow 2021 was to salvage nature, its endangered creatures, humanity, and the works of humanity, wherever they may be – and in the very long term. This manual proposes only that those who follow its recommendations will lead relatively pleasant and meaningful lives for a generation or two – and perhaps three.

Is that too limited? Not at all! It is virtually utopian! History shows that three generations and the century they span are an eternity in human affairs. Furthermore, think of this: the promise for a nice week, which is rare, is here exceeded by the proposal of a nice life!

This is a book for realists who require a rare kind of spirit – one which understands the balance between the possible and the necessary. It will be necessary to have a new kind of local government, one that is much more efficient with implementation and agile in its decision-making. They must also understand that things will fall apart gradually. Yet, even then, sustaining life for a while will be worthwhile compared with the collapse that will inevitably occur elsewhere.

One last note: this book is not the only one you need. Make reference to the masterful volume by David Fleming called *Lean Logic* and to the movement that it catalyzed called Transition Town. With this book in your hand, you are not alone.

Andrés Duany

ACKNOWLEDGMENTS

Urbanism provides answers to many questions that environmentalists raise. This has been my observation since the early 1990s when I conducted my studies for my doctorate degree at the Institute for Environmental Studies, University of Wisconsin, Madison. That's also when I was first exposed to New Urbanism through a lecture by Andrés Dunay and a DPZ charette conducted at Middleton, a suburb of Madison, Wisconsin. Achieving sustainability through good urbanism has been an overarching objective that has given direction to my teaching, research, and practice since then.

When Andrés approached me at CNU 28, in Louisville, Kentucky, June 2019, and invited me to work with him and Paul on the subject of adaptation, I considered this invitation a gift. My relationship with Andrés has been very similar to a relationship of an advisor and a dissertator. Even though I ended up putting this book together, many of the ideas presented here have been developed between us. When I started working with him, there were already many ideas on the table: subsidiarity as a necessary principle for localization and centrality of a new generation of urbanism in developing a practical approach to adaptation. We agreed about the merits of focusing on adaptation, not mitigation, as intellectually the most sensible direction in the face of the climate crisis. Even though there were many discussions within CNU circles, especially after the CNU Climate Summit that took place in Alexandria, Virginia, September 2017, we, the new urbanist community, lacked a comprehensive framework of how urbanists could contribute to, and facilitate, adaptation.

In order to jump start our efforts and develop a new development model, I invited Andrés to a 3-day workshop in my office, Pel-Ona Architects and Urbanists, in Boulder, Colorado, in February 2020. Peter Swift, as well as my business partner Ronnie Pelusio and CNU Colorado Chapter President Alexander Person, joined us in this workshop. My employees, Melissa Harrison, Matt Johnson, Daniel Sailor, and Caresa Atencio, and my students, Ryan Handy and Alex Hemmer, attended and helped us as well in designing an initial version of the adaptation village presented in this book. The workshop was finalized with a presentation at the University of Colorado Boulder, on February 15, 2020. I sincerely express my gratitude to the hard-working team of this workshop.

With the discussions of the workshop fresh in our minds, Andrés and I had an intense half hour of brainstorming in my car as I was driving him to the airport, on the morning of February 16, which produced the three-legged adaptation framework (the one presented in Table 1.1) that provides the structure of this book.

The Boulder workshop was followed by the 3-day California Adaptation Forum initiated by Andrés and organized by CNU California, in early March (just before we cancelled all our travels because of the COVID-19 pandemic). Some of the earlier versions of the ideas included in this book were presented there. The discussions in the forum were helpful in expanding my thoughts and clarifying some of the arguments of this book to myself. If I cannot explain and justify them in simple terms, that means I myself am not clear about the directives. These discussions have been ongoing, intensely, via several new urbanist email groups focusing on adaptation. Although there are many who have been contributing to the exchange of ideas, I would like to name a few: John Anderson, Scott Bernstein, Howard Blackson, Laura Clemons, Steve Coyle, Ann Daigle, Bruce Donnelly, Douglass Farr, Sara Hines, Andy Kunz, Douglass Kelbaugh, Matt Lambert, Michael Mehaffy, Steve Mouzon, Fernando Pagés Ruiz, Lynn Richards, Sandy Sorlien, and Scott Watkins. I thank them for keeping my critical mind awake.

Paul Crabtree's ideas, edits, and advice have been instrumental in developing many of the arguments in this book, especially those regarding the localization of sustenance systems. I express my sincere gratitude.

Writing a book that covers the subjects of many disciplines is a challenge, and the help of a creative editor is valuable. Nancy Bruning has been that person for this book; she went through several edits to make the text flow well, with a consistent tone. Thank you, Nancy. My hiring of Nancy has been made possible via financial help provided by the Vinyl Siding Institute (VSI), an institution that has become a good friend of the new urbanists in recent years. Thank you, VSI.

I would like to extend my gratitude to Routledge and my editor at Routledge, Kathryn Schell. She has been patient with me as I missed several deadlines and changed the outline of the book.

I saved the best for the last. That this book could not have been realized without Andrés Duany is an understatement. Not only did he collaborate in developing the backbone of this book's arguments, generously giving me many ideas and even editing my language, but he also let me write this book and put my name on it. I, the student, salute you as the master, with my deepest gratitude.

1
THE APPROACH

As planners and urbanists, we have the responsibility to expect the worst and plan for it. We are entering an era of climate disasters. We are past most of the tipping points to mitigate greenhouse gas emissions. The political will to change the patterns of human activity at the requisite global scale is limited. Various unprecedented challenges crowd our future. Where and how will we live, in this increasingly unrecognizable, unpredictable, difficult world?

This book is a manual that outlines a set of principles and techniques to enable a built and natural landscape adapted to the difficult future we face. It is a comprehensive proposal of adaptation via localization. It demonstrates how to secure systems that sustain life (energy, water, food, waste, and production of essential goods) as well as political and social protocols enabling agile decision-making to manage these systems effectively at local scales. It also provides the design principles for creating a built environment that will enable the kind of localization we need for adaptation.

This book shows how it is possible to create a life that does not depend on large-scale regional sustenance systems which are likely to be disrupted or fail. We show how to enable people to be creative, productive, and supportive at local levels, so that we can achieve strong and diverse local economies that can sustain life. Localization of sustenance systems, adopting governance models together with the appropriate social organizations, and the design principles for the right urban environment that can enable

DOI: 10.4324/9781003182627-1

1

Table 1.1 The Action Framework for Adaptation

EQUILIBRIUM IN LOCALIZATION (Overarching objective) + ENABLING RELOCATION (CHAPTER 4)		
SUSTENANCE SYSTEMS (CHAPTER 5)	SOCIAL ORGANIZATION AND GOVERNANCE (CHAPTER 6)	DESIGN PRINCIPLES (CHAPTER 7)
Energy	Subsidiarity	Nesting
Water	Sharing	Transect
Food	Giving	Succession
Waste	Enjoyment	Gathering
Goods		Secure place
		Climate conscious design

localization are the three legs of the action framework proposed by this book (see Table 1.1).

The first, overarching objective listed in Table 1.1, "equilibrium in localization," emerges from the natural law that states that the more diverse the life within a landscape patch, the more resilient it is to disturbances. This is one of the fundamental principles of ecology, and the same principle holds for economics and the health of social life. Diversity must be in balance locally. Too much of one thing, "putting all the eggs in one basket," exposes a place and makes it vulnerable to large fluctuations. A practical framework is needed to monitor and calibrate the many facets of a community as it approaches and sustains a balanced self-sufficiency. In ecology, this is known as equilibrium. Thus, we suggest "equilibrium in localization" as an overarching objective for adaptation. Localism is the platform of resilience. Most of the adaptation action, therefore, is within the specific local scale of urbanism. Although attractive in itself, localism is at odds with various facets of our current production and political systems, and it will not be easy to make a full transition. But the rolling disaster of climate change will force its emergence and prove its usefulness.

The second objective of the action framework of adaptation is "enabling relocation." A new generation of comprehensive plans needs to be crafted. These plans need to establish "receiving zones" designed to enable moving to more localized and resilient lifestyles. Even though moving away from danger is the most sensible response to the upcoming disasters, in this economy, where real estate provides the primary wealth for an average household, letting go of a property in a risk zone is not an easy option. The pressure on politicians to finance rebuilding is immense. When the value of the property is lost, the burden lies on the shoulders of the private owner. It is, however, our responsibility, as planners and urbanists, to enable relocation as an attractive option. Instead of having forced relocation as the only option, good planning proactively provides other attractive options.

There are other impediments to relocation. Since the late 1920s, the zoning system has focused on protecting single-family detached houses by separating them from other uses and creating the single-use neighborhoods we now call suburban sprawl. Car-dependency, separation of various uses, and an isolated monoculture social life are primary properties of sprawl. The consequences include social distancing of the various segments of the society from each other, as well as exclusion of life-sustaining services from neighborhoods. These qualities are the antithesis of diversity and self-sufficiency. The recent decades of disasters have revealed that these areas suffer the most, whereas urban areas with complexity and a pedestrian social structure respond to crises more effectively. The social distancing that evolved with the desire to protect low-density residential neighborhoods from the disturbances brought by other land uses shaped another characteristic of the cultural landscape of the United States: disdain for strangers. In most localities today, the idea of creating receiving zones to invite people from other areas to move in will attract a serious negative reaction, making its realization politically difficult, if not impossible.

A new generation of planning needs to be initiated to enable both rational localization of sustenance systems and encouragement to relocate from high-risk areas. This is why mobilization and localization efforts need to be comprehensive and should involve regional coordination. At the very least, this means proactively withdrawing rebuilding funds from areas we know will be destroyed again and instead investing in receiving areas to create resilient lifestyles of the future. The enabling needs to be initiated at the federal and state levels to be widespread, fast, and comprehensive. The Standard State Zoning Enabling Act (1924) and the Standard City Planning Enabling Act (1928) provide not only inspiration but also a good template of how this can be achieved. These Acts showed the states how to delegate to local government the power to regulate the use of land. They have changed the planning culture effectively, even though it is now obvious to us that first-generation zoning fostered a land use pattern, as mentioned above, that is not resilient in the face of climate disasters. What needs to be underlined here is the effectiveness of these Acts in initiating and structuring a new local planning culture where many land use and urban development decisions are made by cities, villages, and towns. Another useful example of such an initiative aiming at enabling local decision-making is the EIS (Environmental Impact Statement) requirement of the NEPA (National Environmental Protection Act, 1970), which is a federal directive that enables local nongovernmental organizations to scrutinize the impact of projects.

Enabling relocation creates a unique opportunity to transform our urban and rural landscapes towards more resilient living. Receiving zones create a framework in which to craft useful policies and programs, including the following four essential ones (which are explored in detail in Chapter 4): (a) create and encourage more productive ownership models via solutions such as compounds; (b) establish preferential tax treatment, such as opportunity zones, to diversify the new local economies; (c) adopt tax deduction programs for rent for those breadwinners who live close to their work and rent from an owner who lives on the same lot; and (d) provide government subsidies for localized infrastructure. Any FEMA funding for resilience, such as the expensive but futile building of sea walls where severe storms are expected in the near future, should instead be channeled into establishing or upgrading the infrastructure in designated receiving areas.

Creating resilience via self-sufficiency is essential. But what should be the scale? Here we suggest achieving self-sufficiency within the walking shed as a target. This may be ambitious but necessary. Thus, this book studies practical technologies for the localization of the systems that sustain life (energy, water, food, waste, and production of the essential goods) within the walking shed. This needs to be supported by a social organization, governance, and ownership system guided by the principles of subsidiarity, sharing, giving, and enjoyment. This kind of community needs an urban environment – what we call an adaptation village – that supports localization and the social order such localization necessitates. The design principles for achieving an adaptation village are nesting, gathering, transect, succession, secure place, and climate-conscious design.

This book is written as a manual aimed at providing practical directives for adaptation. The outline follows the action framework presented in

Table 1.1. Before moving onto the directives, however, the question of "why adaptation instead of mitigation in the first place?" is addressed in Chapter 2 via a summary of the recent climate science findings showing us that the likelihood of stopping or reversing global warming, because we are past most of the tipping points, is so small that it is not practical for us planners and urbanists to consider as a realistic option.

Chapter 3 introduces the adaptation village, the exemplary settlement model, as a prelude to the following four chapters. The adaptation village model offers the right environment for localization; it offers nesting of sustenance systems and distills the social order and design principles.

Chapter 4 focuses on enabling relocation and proposes creating adaptation-oriented comprehensive plans that establish "receiving zones." To enable moving away from danger for more resilient lifestyles within the receiving zones, the comprehensive plans need to show strong commitment to the adaptation action framework provided in Table 1.1. Even though these plans may be crafted by cities, counties, or current regional councils or governments today, an initiative of the federal government and states can accelerate a more widespread and comprehensive movement. Such an initiative needs to formulate a few additional policies that can create resilience fast within receiving zones. The chapter proposes four policies: productive ownership, creating opportunity zones, adopting tax-deduction programs for rent, and subsidizing localized infrastructure.

Chapter 5 focuses on the first leg of the adaptation action framework and reviews available technologies for localization of sustenance systems: energy, water, food, waste, and production of essential hard goods. This review uses the scales of the building, compound, block, quadrant, and walking shed. The chapter refers to the high-tech versus low-tech discussion and suggests a new paradigm in engineering: local technology, both high and low.

Chapter 6 focuses on the second leg of the adaptation action framework: governance, ownership, and social organization. It introduces the principle of subsidiarity, which enables governance and ownership models corresponding to the compound, block, quadrant, and walking shed. This chapter reviews examples of organizational structures and emphasizes the importance of achieving symbiosis between place, governance, and society. It explains how sharing, giving, and enjoyment are prerequisites for an effective social order that corresponds to the localization of sustenance systems.

Chapter 7 focuses on the third leg of the adaptation action framework: the design principles of nesting, transect, succession, gathering, secure place, and climate-conscious design. Nesting is a general principle that addresses sustenance and governance systems, as well as spatial organization. It calls for site plan components that nest one within the other; these components are, from smallest to largest: buildings, compounds, blocks, quadrants, and the walking shed. Transect, a cross section from urban to rural, has been a well-utilized organizing principle among many urban planners in the last few decades. The chapter argues that it is also a useful organizing tool for the adaptation village model. Succession refers to the incremental change towards more synergistic relations that needs to occur when a settlement matures. Succession needs to be planned as part of the development model to provide choices for the future decision makers. Gathering calls for places where residents can easily come together and interact. Each component – compound, block, quadrant, and village – needs its own "heart," its own center where gathering is enabled. Secure place underlines the need for simple measures that can be taken at the compound, block, quadrant, and village scales, in order to increase security at times when it will be needed. Finally, the principle of climate-conscious design suggests creating comfort zones within the built environment without depending on mechanical cooling and heating.

Chapter 8 looks forward and considers life in the 21st century. It reviews certain lessons that we have learned from our experience of living with a pandemic and discusses the implications of these lessons for adaptation strategies. Certain changes imposed by the distancing and quarantine requirements will likely have lasting effects. The chapter focuses on three trends: working from home, podding (forming social groups of trust), and contact tracing. It examines these trends and underlines the role of trust in achieving resilience and how it relates to the principles of subsidiarity and nesting exemplified in the adaptation village.

Chapter 9 reviews the primary directives of this book and lays out the road map for enabling adaptation. It defends the concept of self-sufficiency as a target that calls not for exclusivity, but for diversity, equity, and inclusion.

The two appendices provide additional insight for those interested in further discussion. Appendix A introduces some essential tools for crafting the regulatory structure that is necessary for supporting and enabling the adaptation village model. It provides essential definitions, rules, and regulatory measures for adoption within zoning codes. It also discusses the procedural structure of the appropriate regulation culture that can be an integral part of a governance system. It emphasizes the importance of subsidiarity with the kind of dynamic regulatory culture that can foster agility and succession in the adaptation village.

Appendix B provides further discussion on select adaptation terms via brief essays. It is crafted to be a self-standing document that examines these terms and discusses how they relate on various levels to the items of the adaptation action framework proposed by this book.

2

WHY ADAPTATION?

We tend to resist hearing information that threatens the way we live. Confronted with evidence that challenges our hope, or our worldview, we tend to ignore it.

We knew beyond a doubt that cigarette smoking had fatal consequences as early as the mid-1950s. Yet not for decades did it become socially unacceptable. It was not until 1964 that the surgeon general issued a statement linking smoking to health risks, and not until 1992 that the sale of tobacco products to minors was prohibited. Why the delay? Here is what happened. As soon as the tobacco industry heard about the new research threatening the future of sales, as early as 1953, the industry formed the Tobacco Industry Research Committee to sponsor and finance research to challenge the effects of smoking. For years this committee conducted anti-regulation propaganda and used research findings selectively to manipulate the message. There are two important lessons to be learned from the history of smoking. The first lesson is that it is hard to reach enough consensus for change when there are strong business interests invested in obscuring scientific evidence and influencing political discourse and legislation. The second lesson is that change does come eventually, nevertheless.[1]

Like the effects of smoking, the climate crisis is something we don't want to hear about. Unlike smoking, the damage goes beyond personal health, and we don't have the luxury of "eventually." Unlike any other

DOI: 10.4324/9781003182627-2

problem we have faced in history, climate change is on a global scale, and addressing it requires global action. Although we have known about the effects of increasing greenhouse gasses in the atmosphere for a long time, we haven't seen much success in creating an international political consensus for strong action. Now, there is no time left. We need to accept the fact that we will not avoid flood, drought, fire, and windstorm. We need to prepare ourselves. The oceans will neither provide food nor remove carbon. Ecologies will degrade with the dwindling of keystone species such as bees and plankton. Soil will lose its fertility significantly. Major infrastructure systems, such as those that transport energy, water, food, and goods, are likely to be undermaintained. There is no doubt that we will experience deep deficits in energy, water, and food, with the consequences of starvation, migration, economic collapse, disease, and breakdown in institutions that sustain justice, education, the economy, and security. We have already experienced how one failure triggers further failures as complex systems break down.[2] We will see large migrations of many animal species as well as human populations. Many of these moves will be fast, desperate, and unplanned. There is nothing comforting about imagining the horrifying details, yet we need to. Facing these facts is the first step in exploring adaptation.

This chapter has two objectives. The first is to present the dire possibilities and convince us that the likelihood of a miracle to reverse it all is so small that waiting for it is not only unpractical but also disruptive. We need to assume that a miracle will not happen, and the outcome will not be okay. There is no "back to normal," and there is no preserving the life we have been living. To that end, this chapter provides a summary of the evidence of climate science. It might be possible to slow down the collapse and mitigate the harm, but certain processes at this point are irreversible. The second objective of this chapter is to convince us that we need to think in terms of adaptation to the new conditions of a disintegrating ecology. We need to expect the worst and get ready for it. Creating places such as the adaptation village presented in the next chapter is one way of providing conditions that can support life – despite this dismal future – if we, or at least some of us, are to continue with a life that is pleasant enough to be worth living. Crafting the principles of a new kind of urbanism that can guide us to create these conditions needs to be our highest priority.

Global Warming Effects

Of all the crises the world is facing, climate crisis has the power to worsen all the others. The climate crisis is the result of global warming. Humans have evolved with an atmosphere that regulates its temperature within tight limits. As the solar radiation reaches the planet, some of the energy reflects off the surface back into space; some gets absorbed by the atmosphere and warms the planet. The fragile balance between what is reflected and what is absorbed sustains the temperatures that support life. The atmosphere holds the heat via greenhouse gasses, much like the glass in a greenhouse. The primary greenhouse gasses are carbon dioxide (CO_2), methane (CH_4), nitrous oxide (N_2O), ozone (O_3), and water vapor (H_2O).[3]

There are many crucial feedback loops in environmental systems that sustain life-supporting conditions via fragile balances. The way our atmosphere regulates temperature is one of these. If one or more of the factors change, such as an increase in greenhouse gasses, the feedback loop becomes an amplifying cycle, a cycle that disrupts the balance. There is ample data proving that this is happening with the climate. We have been disrupting the balance because of the greenhouse gasses produced by our activities, including power generation, transport, farming, and industry. According to NASA, CO_2 levels alone have increased by about 50 percent since the Industrial Age began 250 years ago, and CH_4 has doubled.[4] Hence, the increase in average global temperatures.

We have now reached the threshold of a 1.5°C increase in global temperatures since the Industrial Age. According to the Intergovernmental Panel on Climate Change (IPCC), further amplification of this cycle is likely, and the consequences will be dire.[5] The 2020 IPCC report, prepared by a group of 67 scientists, documents:

> Warming has resulted in an increased frequency, intensity and duration of heat-related events, including heatwaves in most land regions (*high confidence*). Frequency and intensity of droughts has increased in some regions (including the Mediterranean, west Asia, many parts of South America, much of Africa, and north-eastern Asia) (*medium confidence*) and there has been an increase in the intensity of heavy precipitation events at a global scale (*medium confidence*).
>
> (IPCC 2020, p. 9)

The most up-to-date IPCC report, issued on August 9, 2021, echoes this observation, but it claims that the effects are further intensifying:

> Human-induced climate change is already affecting many weather and climate extremes in every region across the globe. Evidence of observed changes in extremes such as heatwaves, heavy precipitation, droughts, and tropical cyclones, and, in particular, their attribution to human influence, has strengthened since AR5 [the 2020 report].
>
> (IPCC 2021, p. 10)

The ocean is one of the largest of the balancing systems. It absorbs heat from the sun, as well as CO_2 from the atmosphere. When the layer of heated surface water reaches a certain thickness, as has started to happen, the circulation that mixes the surface layer with the deeper waters diminishes. The ability of the ocean to absorb CO_2 then decreases for two reasons. First, the higher concentration of CO_2 in the atmosphere means the surface water is already saturated with CO_2. Second, the surface water cannot lower its CO_2 concentration because the thickness of the hot surface layer limits circulation. This lessens the ocean's capacity to support critical marine organisms such as plankton; plankton are at the base of the food chain and they are critical in supporting marine and freshwater food webs. Beyond the nutritional implications, plankton use photosynthesis and convert CO_2 to O_2. Phytoplankton in particular are responsible for up to half of the O_2 we breathe. Thus, a decrease in plankton further diminishes the ocean's ability to absorb CO_2.[6] This is an amplifying cycle. The evidence is increased acidity and decreased marine life.

The way snow and ice reflect back much of the solar energy into space is a significant part of the feedback loop that sustains the temperature range that supports life on the planet. Increasing temperatures melt the snow and ice and expose darker surfaces that absorb more heat, which amplifies the warming. Permafrost, which refers to the year-round ice-rich soil, can be up to 260 feet deep in the Arctic. As it thaws, dormant microbes decompose the organic matter, which releases CO_2 and CH_4 into the atmosphere, contributing to further warming.[7] Also, as the polar ice sheets melt, the water-level rise causes flooding along shoreline communities. This cycle holds nature and economics in a disastrous embrace: melting ice, permafrost, CH_4, rising sea levels, coastal urban flooding, insurance withdrawing, real estate collapsing, and refugees migrating away from shores.

Another example of an amplifying feedback loop is the degradation and erosion of soil because of a cycle of droughts, rains, and fires. A sequence of such events occurred between 2012 and 2018 along the California coast. A prolonged drought was followed by extreme precipitation, resulting in excess growth of shrubs and tall grasses. A hot summer followed, which dried the new vegetation. Record-breaking winds, together with the dry vegetation, created large-scale fires. These were followed by heavy rainfall over the burned area, causing some of the worst landslides in California's history, killing 23 people, and damaging more than 400 homes.[8] Such a sequence of events has become common in many other locations around the globe.

Desertification is another form of fertile soil degradation. There is drastic and overall desertification in many regions of the globe. Some of this results from increasing temperatures, and some is also caused by direct human activity, such as clear-cutting in the rainforests of the Amazon. The 2020 IPCC report highlights "shifts of climate zones in many world regions, including expansion of arid climate zones ... As a consequence, many plant and animal species have experienced changes in their ranges, abundances, and shifts in their seasonal activities" (IPCC 2020, p. 10).[9]

These climate-related amplifying cycles are the primary ones. It is relatively easier to identify, measure, and make projections about them. There are also other prospective threats caused by a web of changes triggered by these primary amplifying cycles. They are more complex threats and harder to make projections about.

A Fuller Picture

Increase in the frequency and intensity of storms and floods affects our ability to maintain our infrastructure of roads, bridges, railroads, subways, and the electrical grid. For instance, we depend on aged large-scale water and waste systems in many coastal parts of the country; these are vulnerable in the face of floods. Their failure contaminates the soil and water reserves needed for drinking, crop irrigation, and so on.

In a ripple effect, global warming will cause further changes in societal configurations. For example, many of the catastrophic events we have experienced already have increased or created poverty, assuring social unrest. A report by the United Nations Human Rights Council states:

> Climate change will have devastating consequences for people in poverty. Even under the best-case scenario, hundreds of millions will face food insecurity, forced migration, disease, and death.
> (United Nations Human Rights Council 2019, p. 1)

Such interconnected impacts of climate change are complex and are outside of this book's scope. The intention here is to provide a brief review of the published evidence. Nobel Prize-winning climate scientist Burton Richter discusses the prospects in his book, *Beyond Smoke and Mirrors: Climate Change and Energy in the 21st Century* (2014). In order to provide a comprehensive list of the possible threats mentioned by Richter in his book, Paul Crabtree created a table that is included here (Table 2.1). When it comes to climate crisis, it has been our observation that each bit of good news is followed by a "but," hence the column headings "good news" and "bad news" in Table 2.1.

Waiting for a Miracle

According to Andrés Duany, there are two kinds of climate change denialists: (a) those who deny that global warming is happening, and, even if it is, that human activity is causing it; and (b) those who deny that it is too late to mitigate the impacts of climate change. Both groups cause distraction from focusing on developing strategies for adaptation while we still have some time.[10]

There is an old parable about a town that evacuates because of an impending flood. The priest is the only holdout. As the waters rise, he clings to the bell tower. He refuses first rescue by the fire brigade. Then, as the waters rise, he refuses rescue by the Navy. When only the belfry remains above the waters, he refuses a helicopter rescue. "No," he says each time. "A miracle will happen and God will save me because I am protecting his house." And so, he dies. Meeting God he says, "You let me down." Flabbergasted, God says: "I sent the fire rescue for you, I sent the boats, and I even sent a helicopter, what else did you expect?"

We are at the bell tower. There is no grand miracle coming to mitigate climate change. It is time to expect the worst and prepare for it. We are on our own. This is perhaps the first of many publications that deny the

Table 2.1 Good News and Bad News: A Critical and Selective Summary of *Beyond Smoke and Mirrors: Climate Change and Energy in the 21st Century* (Richter 2014), prepared by Paul Crabtree

GOOD NEWS	BAD NEWS
1. Sun power incident to the Earth is equivalent to the energy output of 100 million large electricity generating plants.	1. Collecting the sun power has massive impacts on land use, and solar pv has ~20% efficiency due to intermittent sunlight and weather conditions.
2. The greenhouse effect has the beneficial effect of balancing the average temperature of the Earth from freezing to about 18 degrees centigrade.	2. Without the greenhouse effect, the average temperature of the Earth would be around 0 degrees centigrade. But too much greenhouse effect raises the temperature higher than it's been in millennia.
3. Human existence has spanned many ice ages and civilizations have moved around to where climatic conditions were tolerable.	3. Now there are seven billion humans going on ten billion and moving that many people is not feasible.
4. The earth naturally removes greenhouse gases (GHG) from the atmosphere.	4. The natural removal rate of greenhouse gasses (GHG) is measured in centuries, and the atmospheric concentration of GHG will not even start to reduce until human emissions have ceased.
5. The sulfates emitted from burning coal contribute to cloud formation, which reduces climate forcing.	5. The sulfates that help form clouds result in acid rain.
6. Fluorocarbons are a potent GHG that were a serious threat in the 70's but were quickly curbed because substitutes were readily available, the number of offenders were few, and economic implications were small.	6. For GHG, what to do is not so clear, the offenders are virtually everyone, and the economic implications are large.
7. The ocean absorbs CO_2, taking GHG out of the atmosphere.	7. The ability of the oceans to absorb CO_2 decreases as ocean temperatures rise; and the oceans are acidifying.
8. The land absorbs CO_2, taking GHG out of the atmosphere.	8. The land absorbs CO_2 steadily but very slowly.
9. Plants remove roughly 100 Gigatons of CO_2 from the atmosphere annually.	9. Plants return roughly 100 Gigatons of CO_2 from the atmosphere annually.
10. The CO_2 increase that causes the earth to warm also results in additional plant growth that removes CO_2 from the atmosphere.	10. Deforestation presently exceeds afforestation.
11. Geoengineering by putting sulfate aerosols into the upper atmosphere could reduce global warming by reflecting sunlight back into space. Volcanic eruptions do this naturally.	11. The unintended negative consequences of geoengineering have not been sufficiently studied; and large-scale interventions can have large-scale unintended consequences.
12. Seeding the ocean with iron could spur plankton growth that would remove CO_2 from the atmosphere and transport it to the ocean bottom.	12. Recent experiments at iron-seeding have not worked, and unintended consequences are unknown.
13. In Earth's lifetime changes in temperature, GHG concentration, and sea level have occurred that dwarf any of the changes being discussed now. Earth will be fine.	13. Today's GHG levels are causing major geological effects that no humans (100,000 years) or human civilizations (10,000 years) have experienced.
14. The Vostok ice cores provide a reliable history of 420,000 years of Earth's CO_2 levels and temperatures; and show that Milankovitch cycles (orbital variations) dominated as the cause of glacial and interglacial periods (not GHG concentrations).	14. In the last 420,000 years the temperatures varied only from 5 F°/3 C° warmer and 14 F°/8 C° cooler than today, while GHGs varied from 190 ppm to 300 ppm. We have exceeded 410 ppm – a rapid change on the geological scale. And the natural trend is for slow cooling and rapid warming.

CLIMATE CRISIS

EMISSIONS AND ACTION

GOOD NEWS	BAD NEWS
1. Argument: Our energy consumption is high but that there is no need for panic. We will find new energy resources.	1. Counter-argument: Climate change consequences are so severe as to constitute a global emergency and that drastic action is called for immediately.
2. The burning of fossil fuels produces cheap reliable energy that is vital to the survival of the human race.	2. The burning of fossil fuels creates externalities that are not accounted for in the price of the energy created.
3. The earth's natural resources have the potential to supply many times the Total Primary Energy Supply of mankind. Solar 8000 x, wind 60 x, ocean waves 4x, tides 0.25x, geothermal 2.3x, photosynthesis 6.5x, rivers 0.5x as compared to the 2004 TPES (Total Primary Energy Supply).	3. All that natural energy is not very accessible. Oceans cover 70% of the planet, we cannot absorb all the wind without creating disastrous climate problems, there is no sunshine at night, the wind blows intermittently.
4. Reducing emissions from the energy supply is relatively easy at the start because there are large gains in efficiency to be made.	4. Reducing emissions become progressively harder as emissions are wrung out of the system.
5. An electric car uses no primary energy.	5. An electric car uses secondary energy (electricity) that was made from primary energy sources.
6. We can reduce global GHG emissions while maintaining the same economic output by changing the mix of fuels that we use, and/or use energy more efficiently.	6. World population will increase for at least the next 50 years. The billions of poor of the world will insist/deserve to increase their GPD using cheap reliable energy sources.

FOSSIL FUELS

GOOD NEWS	BAD NEWS
1. The world runs on cheap reliable fossil fuels which have helped create a vastly improved standard of living planet wide.	1. Fossil fuel supplies are a finite resource that will eventually run out. We just don't know when.
2. There is enough known coal, oil and gas to last a good part of this century and the rate at which exploration has added to reserves has exceeded the consumption rate.	2. The cost of fossil fuels is likely to get more expensive, and harder to extract and process, as time goes on, depending on technological advances.
3. Shale gas has become inexpensive due to horizontal drilling, produces 30% as much CO_2 as coal, and is replacing the dirtier-burning coal in the marketplace.	3. Fracking flares off a huge amount of gas, perhaps even enough to offset its advantage over coal.
4. There are massive untapped fossil fuels in the form of methane hydrates that are trapped in arctic and deep oceans.	4. There is presently no commercial-scale gas production of methane hydrates. The production process is likely to release significant amounts methane.
6. The world can reliably continue business-as-usual use of fossil fuels for at least the next fifty years.	6. The profligate use of the known reserves would result in several doublings of GHG concentrations and will eventually run out.
7. There are enough known nuclear reserves to provide virtually carbon-free energy for tens of thousands of years.	7. Many environmentalists fight the development of nuclear plants – making them expensive and unpopular.
8. Due to the shale gas revolution cleaner burning gas is replacing coal plants in the United States.	8. Coal has long been a major source of electricity generation and remains the lowest cost fuel for the rest of the world, and its usage is rising.
9. The life cycle emissions (including mining, transport, plant building, etc) of non-coal or natural gas plants are significantly lower.	9. In spite of this, coal and natural gas power plants continue to provide 70% of the world's power.

(Continued)

CARBON PRICING

GOOD NEWS	BAD NEWS
1. If disposal of the waste (CO_2) were included in the cost of energy, the global GHG emissions rate would change in a flash.	1. Making energy more expensive globally would be a prohibitive hardship on developing countries.
2. The cost of CO_2 emissions could be quantified by determining the cost of carbon capture and storage of the CO_2 emitted by a coal-fired plant.	3. The EU has a carbon emissions market that is quite volatile, and the typical rate is well below the cost of Carbon Capture and Storage (CCS)
3. If Carbon Capture and Storage (CCS) worked, coal with CCS could be used for some time while newer carbon-free technologies mature.	3. CCS uses energy and reduces the efficiency of a power plant. It's unknown how long the CCS storage systems keep the CO_2 out of the atmosphere.
4. New limits on mercury emissions will cause the shut-down of the dirtiest coal-fired plants due to the cost of compliance.	4. The cost of electricity increases, and the plants are mostly being replaced by gas-fired plants.

ENERGY EFFICIENCY AND CONSUMPTION

GOOD NEWS	BAD NEWS
1. Improving energy efficiency is the cheapest and easiest way to reduce GHG emissions.	1. In the last few decades, little has been done to improve energy efficiency.
2. Energy not used reduces imports, emits no GHG and is free.	2. Energy costs have been so low that there has been little consumer or political pressure for energy efficiency.
3. The transportation and building sectors use far more energy than is necessary; thus, it should be easy to reduce the consumption.	3. Nothing since the oil shock of the 1970s OPEC embargo has incentivized consumers or politicians to reduce energy usage.
4. CAFÉ (Corporate Average Fuel Economy) standards enacted in 1975 resulted in a doubling of the average miles per gallon of the US auto fleet.	4. The price of oil dropped precipitously in 1986 and with it came a drop in efforts to improve efficiency.
5. The General Motors EV-1 all-electric car of the late 1990's was 2-3x as efficient as a standard internal combustion engine (ICE) car.	5. GM recalled all the EV-1s in 2002 and crushed them. The automobile industry lobby is still very strong.
6. Only 13% of the energy of an ICE car goes toward moving the car down the road.	6. 60% of the energy consumption of an ICE car is lost in the engine to friction and heat.
7. 55 % of US vehicles travel less than 60 miles per day, so the market segment for hybrid and electric vehicles is high.	7. As of 2016 there were only 2m electric vehicles on the road globally out of a total of 80 million – 2.5%.
8. There is a lot of efficiency that can be gained in the building sector.	8. The building stock grows slowly and turns over slowly – the net number of buildings in the US grows only 1-2 % per year.
9. If we can increase efficiency in buildings 1.5% per year we could stop the growth of building energy usage.	9. Total energy used in buildings has been growing faster than the population since we continue to increase the number of gadgets and appliances that require energy.
10. There are many ways to make buildings more efficient: better insulation, better window coatings, improved efficiency in ACs, white roofs, occupancy sensors, etc.	10. The users haven't been motivated in levels that can make a difference since savings to the individual may be small while savings to society are larger.
11. There are building efficiency programs that have worked well: Appliance standards as initiated by California in 1978. Efficiency programs run by utility companies that are based on decoupling utility profits from sales. Energy-efficient building codes.	11. In implementing appliance efficiencies, the manufacturer's costs go up, and they lose competitive advantage if other manufacturers don't follow suit. Many states have not adopted utility industry decoupling.

GOOD NEWS

1. Large hydropower systems supply close to 18% of the world electricity.

2. Small hydropower development is efficient and has fewer environmental concerns.

3. Wind and solar systems provide close to 4% of US electricity supply. Wind is an ancient power supply and it is free.

4. Global wind power is growing at a fantastic pace exceeding 20% per year globally.

5. Wind power systems have high capacities to produce power. Those are the capacities that are written on the turbine's name plate.

6. Wind systems are a small but growing industry that can reduce GHG emissions compared to conventional fossil fuel powered systems.

7. Solar PV system capacity is increasing, and costs decreasing rapidly, though from a small base.

8. Solar thermoelectric systems have higher efficiencies than solar PV, their tracking systems make more efficient use of sunlight, and they have the potential to store energy as well – as heat.

9. Geothermal power technology is well developed, and new plants are being built wherever there is a good source of hydrothermal energy.

10. Ocean energy has a great potential. The total energy in all the world's waves and tides is four times the TPES.

BAD NEWS

1. Large hydropower systems have potential environmental problems

2. Only a few hydropower sites in the United Stats have been developed.

3. Modern new giant wind turbines are very expensive and are feasible only with tax subsidies.

4. Wind power systems need sites that have steady wind speeds at the turbine's sweet spot.

5. Wind power systems actually produce about 21% of the name plate power due to the variable winds.

6. Wind power can grow to 5 to 10% of the electricity supply with no real problems, but above that level the power grid needs upgrading, and back-up supplies/storage need to be solved.

7. Solar PV capacity is much different from output, which varies greatly depending on latitude and weather.

8. On a lightly overcast day thermoelectric solar systems produce nearly nothing. Also, there is the added cost of steam generation and turbine systems.

9. The cooled wastewater can be loaded with harmful gases and minerals. The water resource is limited and requires a closed cycle where steam and water are pumped back into the aquifer.

10. Only a tiny fraction of wave energy is accessible, and there has been little success in garnering the resource.

RENEWABLES

1. Biofuels can reduce the dependence on imported oil. It is easy to gather and burn natural-grown plant material for cooking and heat.

2. Ethanol derived from plants can be used as a motor fuel as well as for convivial drinking.

3. A Cellulosic ethanol process converts more of the plant material to fuel, and it may be able to use forest waste or other materials that would not affect agricultural lands.

4. Methane captured from landfills and manure ponds can be used as a fuel.

1. In order to respond to the demand farming the biofuels requires extra chemical and energy inputs, and food crops are turned to fuel crops.

2. Corn-based biofuels do not reduce GHG.

3. So far, efforts to scale up cellulosic ethanol production have failed.

4. Methane capture is not much used, even in developed nations.

BIOFUELS

prospect of saving the world as we know it. Let us end this chapter with a quote from Andrés Duany:

> There is little chance to save all humans and most species everywhere and forever. That is an absurd megalomania – even if the situation were not so awful, all we can offer for those who are willing to follow the principles of adaptation is that there will be many good days when life is still worth living for at least a few generations. Is that not an amazing enough prospect?[11]

Notes

1 O'Connor and Weatherall (2019) provide a good summary of the tobacco industry's campaign during the last five decades (see pp. 93–96). See also Oreskes and Conway's (2010) book titled *Merchants of doubt: How a handful of scientists obscured the truth on issues of tobacco smoke and global warming*. For the effects of group pressure in our choices and decision-making, see Asch (1951).

2 For a more detailed yet compact discussion of these prospects, see the introduction to the book *Surviving the future* by David Fleming (2016b). Also see the term *climacteric* (pp. 43–45) in the book *Lean logic* (Fleming 2016a), which is organized as an encyclopedia of terms. If the reader is interested in further discussion, the literature on these prospects is voluminous. To name a few among many, see Richter (2014), Rifkin (2019), and Smil (2019). Also see the IPCC reports that are quoted in this chapter for detailed evidence.

3 For further discussion on greenhouse gasses, see *climate change* (pp. 45–55) in David Fleming's book *Lean logic* (2016a). See also Lovelock (2014), United States Global Change Research Program (2018) and Wallace-Wells (2019).

4 For detailed information about the change in CO_2 levels, please refer to https://climate.nasa.gov/vital-signs/carbon-dioxide/

5 In its 2018 report, the IPCC reports that, as a result of climate-induced impacts, coral reefs, which are already in decline, are projected to decline by a further 70–90% at 1.5°C. The IPCC also states: "The level of ocean acidification due to increasing CO_2 concentrations associated with global warming of 1.5°C is projected to amplify the adverse effects of warming ... impacting the growth, development, calcification, survival, and thus abundance of a broad range of species, for example, from algae to fish" (IPCC 2018, pp. 8–9).

6 Plankton's role in the production of O_2 is significant; they are responsible for up to half of the O_2 we breathe; see Spencer (2019).

7 For a detailed discussion of this phenomenon, please see *Unexpected future boost of methane possible from Arctic permafrost*, by Ellen Gray of the NASA Earth Science News Team (2018), which is retrievable from: https://climate.nasa.gov/news/2785/unexpected-future-boost-of-methane-possible-from-arctic-permafrost/

8 For a detailed history and a scientific analysis of these events, please see AghaKouchak et al. (2020).

9 The complete version of the quote reads: "Global warming has led to shifts of climate zones in many world regions, including expansion of arid climate zones and contraction of polar climate zones (high confidence). As a consequence, many plant and animal species have experienced changes in their ranges, abundances, and shifts in their seasonal activities (high confidence)" (IPCC 2020, p. 10).

10 Comment received in person by Andrés Duany.

11 Comment received in person by Andrés Duany.

3

THE ADAPTATION VILLAGE
A DEVELOPMENT MODEL

Leaving behind difficult living conditions and moving towards better possibilities have been important motivational forces that created the westward migration that has shaped American culture since the days of the pioneers and settlers. Moving away from danger is a universal adaptation strategy. Today, however, there are various impediments that make relocation a difficult choice for an average household.

Enabling relocation is one of the primary focuses of this book. Launching the development of a new generation of comprehensive plans that designate receiving zones is an important step to make relocation a financially rational choice for all segments of the society. Creation of receiving zones opens the door for adoption of certain policies as well as for exploration of development models that make life within these zones more resilient. Four such policies will be discussed in the next chapter. Here, we focus on a development model we call the adaptation village.

The adaptation village is a model crafted to substantiate the three-legged adaptation action framework (see Table 1.1). Designation of receiving zones provides an opportunity to create something new and resilient: communities with localized sustenance systems (energy, water, food, waste, and essential goods), which is the first leg. Localizing sustenance systems requires a social order, along with an ownership structure, that enables effective local governance, which is the second leg. This goes hand in hand with development of an urban environment that is created following the design principles of

DOI: 10.4324/9781003182627-3

adaptation urbanism, which is the third leg. We imagine these communities as places where residents are involved in a diverse set of productive activities at various scales, via groups nesting within each other, both in the social and physical environments. In these communities, energy is produced, water is collected, food is grown, and waste is managed within the walking shed. Locals would participate in governance and community life more effectively. Sharing and giving would support conviviality and social interaction. Communities that enable this kind of daily life must, evidently, be different from what we have been building.

This chapter describes the components of the adaptation village as an exemplary development model. It explores spatial organization and circulation systems. It discusses the necessary proximities between land uses, services, and activities that maximize synergies that are essential in diversification of production. It studies spatial organization that supports and encourages neighborly interaction. It explores the geographical distribution of energy production, water storage, food growing, and waste management within the village. It studies building types that can support a variety of social arrangements as well as economic activities, including businesses, from lean start-ups to established services.

An early version of the adaptation village was designed during a brain-storming workshop conducted in Boulder, Colorado.[1] It was proposed as an alternative to a conventional subdivision that was to be annexed to an existing municipality. Annexations are common and popular because they usually join the power grid, receive water from a regional network, and connect to the existing sewage system. However, these large systems are vulnerable to sporadic failures. To remedy this, an adaptation village, even when annexed to an existing municipality, would be designed with a high degree of independence to bridge interruptions in sustenance systems. This is the essence of resilience in the difficult decades to come.

Self-sufficiency within the Walking Shed

The adaptation village demonstrates how a resilient community can be established at the walking shed scale, with all the sustenance systems localized at a level of almost complete self-sufficiency. For the purposes of an adaptation village, the walking shed is defined as a 15-minute walk from one edge of the settlement to the other. This means a circle with a ¾-mile diameter, based on a 3-miles-per-hour average walking speed. Traffic planners usually use a centroidal approach for defining the sheds, where the distance to the center is the primary concern (as in the case of transit stops). However, here, a field approach is used in defining the walking shed for the adaptation village, which is focused on all trips that may happen within the settlement, not only trips to and from the village center. If the adaptation village is truly to be at the walking shed scale, trips to all services, as well as to all neighbors (as part of daily social interaction), located anywhere within the walking shed need to be within a maximum 15-minute walk.

Why 15 minutes? Why not 5 minutes? The 5-minute-walk measure adopted by many transportation engineers as a standard assumes that an average rider would be willing to walk to a transit stop for no more than 5 minutes. However, in many walking-friendly urban environments, residents walk more. Walking to a transit stop is only the first step of the trip, whereas walking to a restaurant or to a friend in the adaptation village would be the entire trip, and as such people would be willing to walk longer. Fifteen minutes is a reasonable measure.[2] It creates a size of settlement that was very common in antiquity, a time when walking was the primary mode of transportation within settlements.

Why a walking shed? Why not biking or driving sheds? As noted previously, we need to expect the worst and plan for it. Gas shortages, power grid failures, and disruptions in regional supplies are among the possible worst-case scenarios of the near future. If we are serious about providing resilience in the face of these possibilities, we need to figure out how to achieve self-sufficiency at the walking shed scale. Even though it is hard to imagine that this can be possible (especially given how dependent on regional networks we are currently), it is nevertheless an achievable goal. In other words, once we realize what life will be like if regional networks are interrupted, even temporarily, the advantages of localization at the walking shed scale become clear. Self-sufficiency at the walking shed scale, however, doesn't prevent the walking shed being nested within biking and driving sheds. Nesting needs to be the case, especially in existing large metropolitan areas. Providing most human needs and desires at biking and driving shed scales still needs to be in our vocabulary of increasing resilience as a target, in addition to reaching a high level of self-sufficiency within the walking shed. Let us emphasize the fact that self-sufficiency at walking shed scale does not prohibit interactions with other mobility sheds – in fact, pockets of self-sufficiencies can and should support and help each other. This is the landscape of a resilient future; this is how we will be able to sustain life when the regional systems are stressed or disrupted.

Size and Density

Even though the village plan should be adjusted to the conditions of the location, the walking shed, which covers an area of approximately 280 acres, is the size at which localization of sustenance systems is targeted. With an additional 140 acres of land for energy production (e.g., solar or wind farm), food production (e.g., intense permaculture), and waste (e.g., composting and treatment), the total reaches around 420 acres.

There is also the density to consider: despite all the advantages, when urban densities approach a certain point, it becomes difficult to employ the localization technologies outlined in this book. Eighteen people per acre, as a gross density, is a recurring number. This might seem low, but the gross density calculation includes thoroughfares, greens, squares, and civic buildings, such as schools and community centers. A gross density of 18 people per acre is the sweet spot: lower densities struggle to create the diversity that is necessary to support a strong local economy; higher densities make it hard to create self-sufficient sustenance systems. Even though dwelling units per acre is not the most accurate way to measure density for the adaptation village model (as will be discussed, most parts of the village accommodate a diversity of uses), it is helpful to provide a number for readers to relate to: at an average of 2.25 people per household, 18 people per acre corresponds to around eight units per acre gross density. This is quite realistic. A 15-minute walking shed of 280 acres can thus accommodate a population of close to 5,000.

Locations

The adaptation village plan presented here is proposed as a new settlement in a peripheral metropolitan location. However, this is not the only place where this model can be applied. Rural locations, including those at a greater distance from established municipalities, would also be candidates – if they meet the mapping criteria for designation as receiving zones (introduced in the next chapter). Depending on the distance from major hubs, villages in these locations may need to form new municipalities, but the model still applies.

The model is also applicable for urbanized infill locations that meet the criteria for receiving zones. The geometry of the plan would respond to the conditions of the specific context, but the basic adaptation village principles would still be relevant. Even though, at walking shed scale, 18 people per acre density works well for employing self-sufficient sustenance sys-

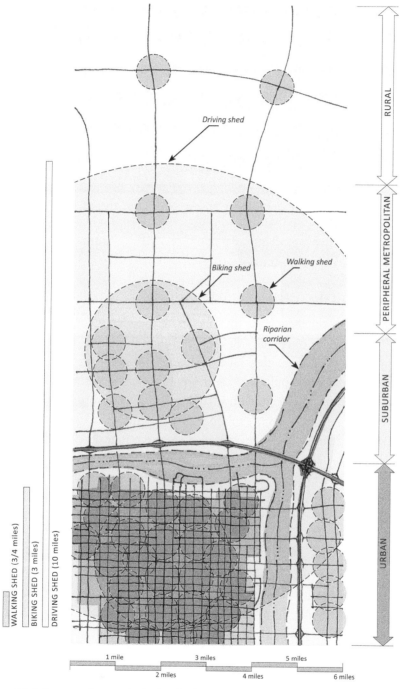

Figure 3.1 A diagrammatic map showing how localization at walking shed scale can achieve pockets of self-sufficiencies within urban, suburban, peripheral metropolitan, and rural contexts. All sheds reflect a 15-minute travel time.

tems, this doesn't mean that we should categorically reject higher densities. Higher densities might not provide the same level of self-sufficiency, but any level of independence makes these communities more resilient. In many established urban neighborhoods, decreasing dependence should be the objective. Consider, for instance, the way urban community gardens provide food and support families living in the middle of urban food deserts. Even though these gardens may not provide food independence, they are a step towards resilience and adaptation. Each move towards self-sufficiency prepares us better for the difficult future.

Figure 3.1 depicts how walking sheds at various locations nest within and interact with other mobility sheds. Note that the existing urban area is divided into several walking sheds, some slightly overlapping each other. This is the vision of a resilient landscape formed by pockets of self-sufficiencies and systems nesting within each other.

Overview of the Adaptation Village

At first glance, the diagrammatic site plan for the adaptation village in Figure 3.2 looks familiar to anyone who has been in a traditional town. Similar to many small-town plans that have evolved in Western history, here as well, civic and commercial buildings are clustered around a centrally located common green at the intersection of two roads. The central green is surrounded by some closely spaced rows of buildings that accommodate a diversity of businesses. Neighborhoods are located in each of the four quadrants and served by what looks like a basic street grid. Although this appears to be conventional, a closer look reveals arrangements that are unique to the adaptation village.

To start, there are many mid-block greens connected to each other, forming a fine-grained network of pedestrian circulation (Figure 3.3). These mid-block greens are surrounded by groups of buildings called compounds. Unlike conventional single-family house lots, compound lots accommodate multiple structures. Compounds have their own courtyards, with various facilities shared by the residents of the compound. Several compounds come together and form blocks, and blocks form quadrants, with larger greens at their centers. These quadrant greens accommodate facilities that serve a larger group of residents. The large linear park located at the center of the village brings together amenities that are shared by the entire village. The civic buildings located at the village center accommodate schools, community functions, libraries, meeting halls, and administrative offices.

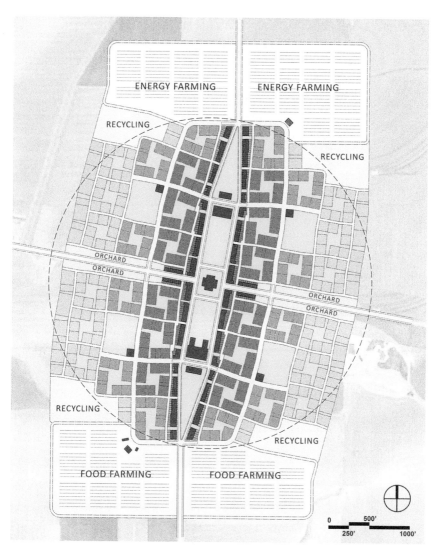

Figure 3.2 The diagrammatic site plan of the adaptation village model. The circle shown indicates the walking shed (3960-foot radius), which is a 15-minute walk from one edge to the other at 3 miles per hour walking speed. This plan accommodates a population close to 5,000 within the walking shed. This corresponds to an average gross density of 18 people per acre.

Another distinguishing characteristic of the adaptation village model is the circulation network of thoroughfares. The only conventional streets on the plan are the two major roads arriving at the village and those circling the central greens. The rest are mews that are shared by pedestrians and

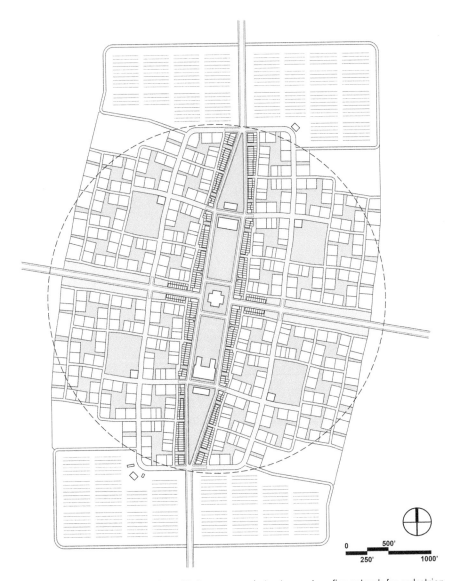

Figure 3.3 Green corridors, together with the mews and streets, create a fine network for pedestrian circulation.

vehicular traffic. Primary mews are relatively wider; they are arranged as linear plazas. Secondary mews are narrower and form a finer grid.

On the plan, there are also large support areas, or districts, which are located outside the walking shed. These are energy and food farms (to the north and to the south), as well as four fields labeled as "recycling," to accommodate leach fields and composting and other recycling facilities.

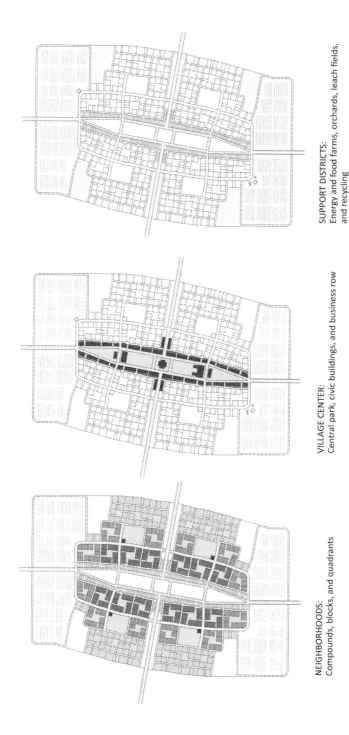

SUPPORT DISTRICTS:
Energy and food farms, orchards, leach fields, and recycling

VILLAGE CENTER:
Central park, civic buildings, and business row

NEIGHBORHOODS:
Compounds, blocks, and quadrants

Figure 3.4 Primary components of the adaptation village.

Figure 3.4 highlights the primary components of the adaptation village: the neighborhoods, village center, and support districts. The rest of the chapter discusses these components in more detail. The chapter closes with a review of how these components are connected by a circulation network formed by streets, primary and secondary mews, and pedestrian pathways.

Neighborhoods

Neighborhoods are formed by quadrants. Moving down in scale, each quadrant consists of blocks that are located around a neighborhood park roughly the same size as a block. Each block consists of compounds and a central green court. These three elements – compounds, blocks, and quadrants – nest within each other. They are the physical basis of the management by subsidiarity (as discussed in Chapter 6).

Compounds

Compounds are the basic building blocks of the adaptation village. They are lots accommodating a cluster of buildings. The compound is a cross-cultural concept common throughout history in support of self-sufficient lifestyles, from the ranchos of the American Southwest to the palazzos of Italy or the hutongs of Beijing. It is multigenerational and multiuse, accommodating a diversity of activities. It is the smallest increment of management, security, and self-sufficiency.

The basic compound lot in the adaptation village is approximately ⅓ acre (drawn on the plans as 120 × 120 feet) and has a capacity of up to six buildings (Figures 3.5 and 3.6). It accommodates various building types, including some suitable as workplaces. The density and composition of the residences vary, depending on the location and the current needs at any given time. Smaller compound lots may be added to the mix to increase diversity by dividing a basic lot into two (to obtain either two lots with dimensions of 60 × 120 feet each or one 80 × 120-feet lot and one 40 × 120-feet lot). The structures may be occupied by a large or extended family, or a family and caregivers, as well as others who rent (for living, for working, or for both). As will be discussed in Chapter 5, single ownership needs to be the predominant form of ownership; this could be a family, a trust, or an association. No entity should be allowed to own more than one such lot. The owner is required to live on the lot in order to be able to rent spaces to others. This is to prevent speculation.

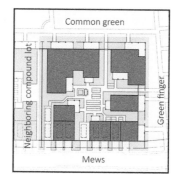

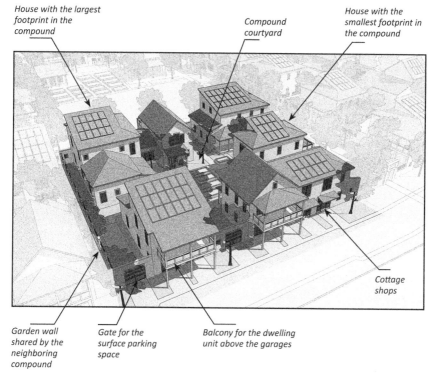

House with the largest footprint in the compound

Compound courtyard

House with the smallest footprint in the compound

Cottage shops

Garden wall shared by the neighboring compound

Gate for the surface parking space

Balcony for the dwelling unit above the garages

Figure 3.5 The lot diagram and a bird's-eye view of a compound with five detached buildings organized around a central courtyard. The compound lot faces the common green to the north (in the background of the perspective), a green finger to the east (on the right), and a mews to the south (in the foreground) and shares a garden wall with the neighboring compound to the west (on the left).

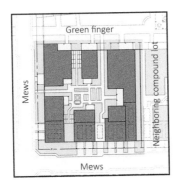

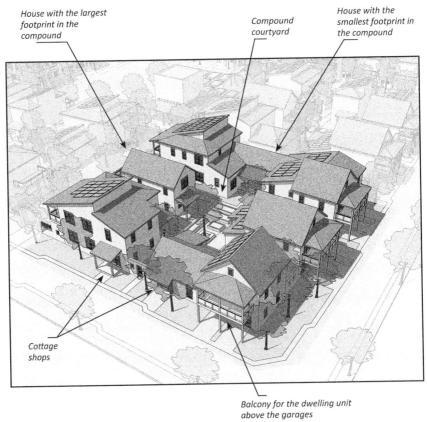

House with the largest footprint in the compound

Compound courtyard

House with the smallest footprint in the compound

Cottage shops

Balcony for the dwelling unit above the garages

Figure 3.6 The lot diagram and a bird's-eye view of another compound with five detached buildings organized around a central courtyard. The compound lot is surrounded by a green finger to the north (upper left), the neighboring compound to the west (upper right), and two mews to the south and to the west (in the foreground).

A compound is a hybrid in its land uses.[3] In addition to residential use, a compound typically accommodates light manufacturing and production, limited retail, and cottage farming.

The compound enables gradual growth and succession. Structures can be added one at a time or remodeled to accommodate new users and uses as needed. It provides financial resilience for the households in two ways: it allows productive activities within the lot and enables renting. Instead of owning a large house and being responsible for all of it on the first day of purchase, which is the case for a typical suburban property, a household can build a small structure on the compound and add others later. Owning the large suburban house is nothing but a liability and a financial burden; it doesn't produce any income. Whereas the compound offers an investment that provides growing return in time via the rental spaces offered and the productive activities accommodated on the lot. The mixture of uses and activities requires limits and controls so that they can coexist harmoniously within the compound and with adjacent compounds. These activities incubate an economy that contributes to the larger scales in which it nests. A dynamic development code is needed to increase synergies. Such a code must evolve as a part of a regulatory culture where the management of local productive activities is merged with code enforcement. The regulatory procedures that guide construction and management need to be based on the principle of subsidiarity. The details of such a code are discussed in Appendix A: Tools for Coding.

Notice how the external spatial arrangement of a compound fosters small business opportunities. Maker spaces, as well as small businesses, can be located in garages or separate small buildings facing the mews. The garages can be designed from the outset to be repurposed as workshops or business spaces as the need for cars diminishes in time. Using separate smaller garage doors instead of a single large one, for instance, provides the opportunity to divide the space (Figures 3.5 and 3.6). Placing generously sized covered balconies above the garage entrances is another simple design solution that creates a more sociable façade along the mews while providing the added safety of "eyes on the street." This is important for a secure and convivial public realm.

The court at the center of the compound is a shared place for the residents of the compound. It plays an important role in daily life. Beyond its utilitarian potential, such as growing food, the courtyard is a gathering place for the residents. Our recent experience with the pandemic has shown that this kind of protected outdoor space is essential for forming groups of trust. The compound model offers a household at a scale larger and looser than the single nuclear family. It supports strong social ties, encourages neighborly interaction, and enables neighbors to see each other as valuable and trusted assets.

Blocks

Several compounds together form the next unit of settlement, the block. Eight basic compounds (120 × 120 feet) are conveniently arrayed around a common outdoor green court (approximately 160 × 160 feet). The court is large enough to accommodate various facilities residents may decide to include. Figures 3.7 and 3.8 show a water tower, a gathering place under the water tower, community gardens, a tool shed, and a common green for games and passive recreation. The water storage in the tower may be fed by a well, a cistern, or another source. Employing water storage in each block significantly increases resilience. Depending on local conditions, other amenities may include mid-sized wind turbines, solar panels, composting facilities, and cisterns.

Figure 3.8 provides a bird's-eye view of a block formed by compounds of various sizes. Even though the basic compound (120 × 120-feet lot) should be the most common size, as mentioned earlier, smaller sizes may also be introduced by dividing the basic lot into two lots (either two 60 × 120-feet lots or one 40 × 120-feet and one 80 × 120-feet lot). This would increase the block's physical and social diversity.

Note that half of the compounds within the blocks are turned 5°, which results in narrowing and widening of the green fingers in trapezoid shapes and a central green in a parallelogram shape. This twist creates a village plan with blocks that are slightly different from each other in size and shape. It also provides more visibility for the building façades in the mews, which is an important factor that not only provides interesting views for pedestrians, but also increases "eyes on the street."

Even though gradual growth with a high level of diversity should be the objective, economy of scale, especially in the early phases of construction, can still be achieved by repeating certain building plans. The challenge is to

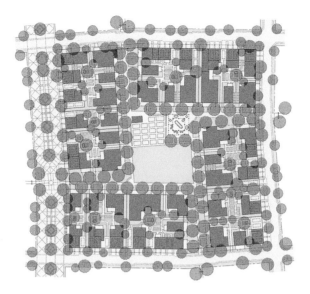

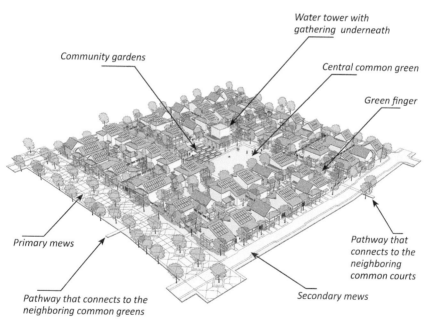

Water tower with
gathering underneath

Community gardens

Central common green

Green finger

Primary mews

Pathway that
connects to the
neighboring
common courts

Pathway that connects to the
neighboring common greens

Secondary mews

Figure 3.7 A diagrammatic plan and a bird's-eye view of an adaptation village block that is surrounded by a primary mews on one side and secondary mews on three sides.

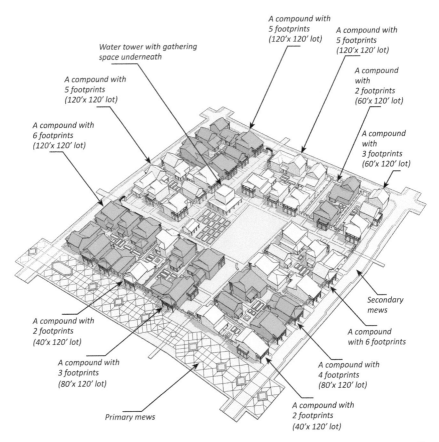

A compound with
5 footprints
(120'x 120' lot)

A compound with
5 footprints
(120'x 120' lot)

Water tower with gathering
space underneath

A compound
with
2 footprints
(60'x 120' lot)

A compound with
5 footprints
(120'x 120' lot)

A compound
with
3 footprints
(60'x 120' lot)

A compound with
6 footprints
(120'x 120' lot)

Secondary
mews

A compound with
2 footprints
(40'x 120' lot)

A compound
with 6 footprints

A compound with
3 footprints
(80'x 120' lot)

A compound with
4 footprints
(80'x 120' lot)

A compound with
2 footprints
(40'x 120' lot)

Primary mews

Figure 3.8 A bird's-eye view of an adaptation village block. Color change indicates the compounds. Five of the compounds are basic 120 × 120-feet lots, two are 80 × 120 feet, two are 60 × 120 feet, and two are 40 × 120 feet.

take advantage of solar gain while facing different directions, which can be achieved with a few plan modifications and specific roof designs for each orientation. Figure 3.9 shows three compounds on the northern, eastern, and southern sides of a common green. The buildings A, B, and C have the same footprints and similar plans, even though their roofs are designed to face south, with solar panels.

Quadrants

Quadrants are formed by blocks located around a neighborhood park that is large enough to accommodate recreational and sports-related facilities, as well as places for gatherings such as concerts, festivals, or weddings. The size of a quadrant is appropriate for an independent sewage system

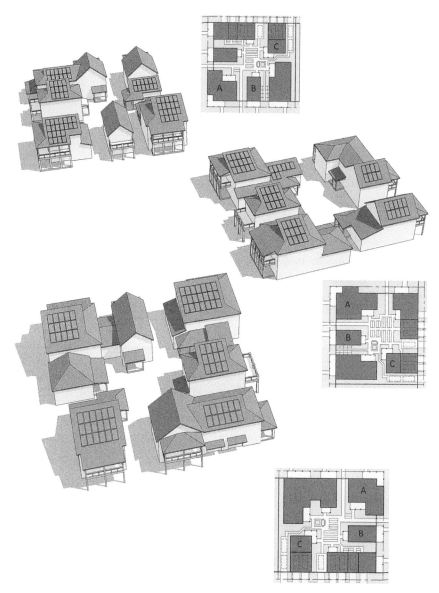

Figure 3.9 Plans and bird's-eye views of three compounds located to the north, to the east, and to the south of a common green. Even though the buildings A, B, and C (which have the same footprint and similar plans) face different directions, their roof design accommodates south-facing solar panels.

to be employed efficiently. It also provides opportunities to establish certain recycling facilities, if they need to be provided at a scale smaller than the entire village. In short, quadrants offer another scale within the nesting continuum of the block and the village.

Village Center

The village center consists of centrally located civic buildings and parks and a row of specialized commercial buildings placed along the central loop, which is the business row. The business row provides the backdrop for the civic buildings so that the civic buildings can claim their foreground status (Figure 3.10).

Civic buildings should be designed as hybrids to support multiple activities and increase synergies between them. This would be in contrast to the gated schools and fenced government buildings that characterize the civic institutions in many of our current town centers. Civic buildings, when isolated, create inefficiencies and foster mistrust. It is common nowadays to observe extreme specialization and isolation in the way we design and manage our civic institutions; we call these single-use, single-purpose buildings civic, yet they contain no civic activities that create and encourage social interaction between different groups. Bringing together various services and activities that target different groups, on the other hand, enhances social contact and strengthens communal management. Halls, for instance, could house many kinds of social functions. Administrative activities also work best when located at social hubs. Schooling faculty and functions, for instance, can be housed in the same building as governmental administrative offices. This would not only create economies in the space, but would also diversify participants' information networks; kids would have contact

Figure 3.10 A bird's-eye view of the village center. In the foreground are the central park, a civic building/ gathering hall (to the left), and a temporary farmers' market; in the background are the business row and neighborhoods. Drawing by Ronnie Pelusio.

with residents of all ages, administrators would have the opportunity to meet parents they wouldn't otherwise meet, and so forth. Considering the population of the adaptation village, it is reasonable to expect that the scale of the civic facilities would be modest. Sharing amenities and creating synergies between facilities become especially critical when the resources are limited. This is the reason why civic buildings need to be hybrid. Also, whenever feasible, civic buildings should expand to an outdoor space such as a courtyard or patio.

The large civic buildings in the village center offer a place for large cisterns. There are also opportunities for small solar or wind farms in the village center (which can reduce the need for energy production that takes place within the support districts). Even though the support districts would hold the larger food farms, modest orchards may be accommodated in the central locations.

The linear organization of the central space allows the successional construction of multiple buildings, of various sizes and in various configurations, as needs evolve. Priority facilities include a library with an advanced computer lab with a semi-independent mesh network. This library could also have a maker place equipped with a laser cutter. This would encourage creative start-up businesses and facilitate the entrepreneurial ecosystem in the community. A centrally located source of information about the productive endeavors and service businesses within the community would be an extension of the administrative office or a coop shop, depending on evolving needs. Also, there needs to be at least one large gathering hall or a barn where a large portion of the town can physically gather for various celebrations and meetings. Special events such as farmers' markets, food and craft fairs, and educational lectures contribute to the awareness of the principles that sustain the adaptation village.

Business Row

Business row is the row of attached buildings facing the streets that loop around the central greens. These house commercial enterprises that range from professional services and neighborhood retail to manufacturing and light industry. The buildings need to be hybrid to flexibly accommodate manufacturing and commercial as well as residential facilities, as these activities support each other.

In order to accommodate and respond to the needs of a wide range of businesses, the business row needs to employ a variety of building prototypes. Figure 3.11 shows four prototypes: the flex space, the hidden court,

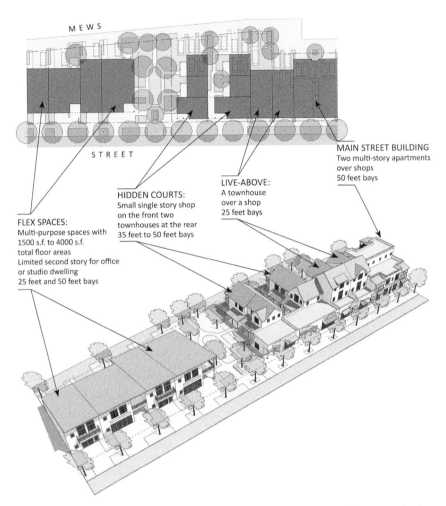

MEWS

STREET

MAIN STREET BUILDING
Two multi-story apartments
over shops
50 feet bays

LIVE-ABOVE:
A townhouse
over a shop
25 feet bays

HIDDEN COURTS:
Small single story shop
on the front two
townhouses at the rear
35 feet to 50 feet bays

FLEX SPACES:
Multi-purpose spaces with
1500 s.f. to 4000 s.f.
total floor areas
Limited second story for office
or studio dwelling
25 feet and 50 feet bays

Figure 3.11 Building types for business row located along the street. These archetypes create strong building presence and support the public realm around the village center parks.

the live-above, and the main street building. Each of these offers a unique lot configuration to accommodate specific needs of different businesses.

Flex space: Flex space buildings offer large, unobstructed ground-floor space for manufacturing activities. Garage doors, both at the front and the rear, provide easy access for loading and unloading and allow some of the creative activities to easily expand outdoors (Figure 3.12). Flex spaces may also function, partly or as a whole, as galleries or show rooms. A mezzanine may accommodate offices or a studio living unit to provide 24-hour presence in the business row. Conceptual architectural drawings for a 25-feet wide and a 37-feet wide flex space are provided in Figures 3.13 and 3.14.

Figure 3.12 An eye-level view towards flex spaces. In the background are a hidden court and a live-above.

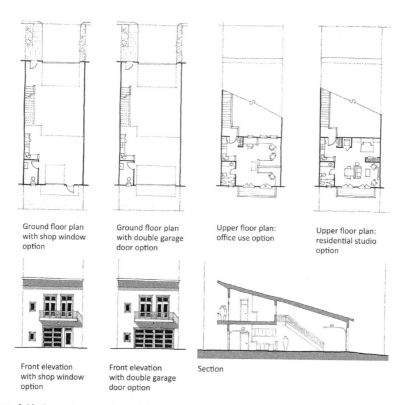

Ground floor plan with shop window option

Ground floor plan with double garage door option

Upper floor plan: office use option

Upper floor plan: residential studio option

Front elevation with shop window option

Front elevation with double garage door option

Section

Figure 3.13 Conceptual architectural drawings of a 25-feet wide flex space.

Ground floor plan

Upper floor plan:
office use option

Upper floor plan:
residential studio option

Front elevation

Section

Figure 3.14 Conceptual architectural drawings of a 37-feet wide flex space.

The hidden court: A hidden court configuration consists of townhouses that face an inner court located behind the front building facing the street. The front building (shown as single story) is appropriate for businesses that would appreciate a high ceiling, including restaurants and shops. The townhouses may be occupied by residential or office users. As they accommodate multiple units, similar to the compound, hidden court lots may offer space for rent.

The live-above: The live-above is a three-story building, essentially a townhouse placed over a commercial ground-floor space, although the upper stories may also be used as offices. The second and third stories are set back from the street, providing physical separation from the sidewalk as well as a terrace, a valuable amenity for a residential unit.

The main street building: The main street building consists of shops on the ground floor with apartments placed over and accessed by an independent staircase (Figure 3.15). Terraces for the residential quarters may be located at the rear over the garages (Figure 3.16).

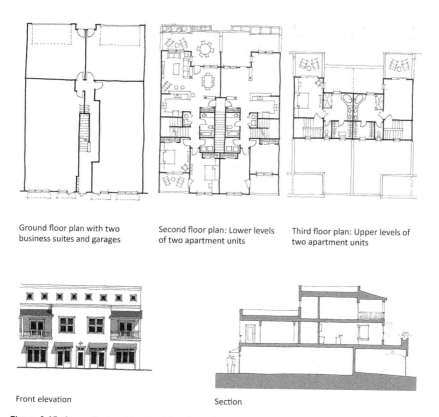

Ground floor plan with two
business suites and garages

Second floor plan: Lower levels
of two apartment units

Third floor plan: Upper levels of
two apartment units

Front elevation

Section

Figure 3.15 Conceptual architectural drawings of a main street building.

Figure 3.16 The rear of the business row buildings along the mews. In the foreground is the main street building, with terraces for apartments located over the garages. Next are two live-above buildings. Next to them are the hidden courts.

These four building types are discussed in further detail in Appendix A: Tools for Coding. Other types are variations of these. Although each type responds to the needs of certain kinds of businesses, all benefit from being in close proximity to each other. They provide the flexibility and reasonably priced space that businesses need to thrive. Their flexibility and reasonable cost allow the diversity of services the community desires. These building types work well together to create an urbanism; they provide a strong presence on the street. They also address the mews and provide a level of conviviality appropriate for transition to the neighborhoods of compounds.

Support Districts

The primary facilities within the support districts are food and energy farms, as well as recycling and waste fields. The amount of land these facilities occupy depends on the availability of sunshine and other renewable resources, as well as the soils and climate of the place. Figure 3.2 shows the food and energy farms occupying an area of approximately 70 acres each. Depending on technology, they may be located separate from each other or they may mix; energy may be produced together with food. An intense solar farm may not be compatible with agriculture, but a wind farm may be. Solar panels placed on greenhouses may produce energy to support the village, in addition to supporting possible grow towers, or hydroponic and aquaponic ponds placed within the greenhouses. In places where the sunshine is consistent, solar panels installed on the rooftops in compounds may produce a significant portion of the energy needed, reducing the intensity and size of the solar farm located within the support district.

The amount of land reserved for support districts shown on the plan in Figure 3.2 assumes intense food production following permaculture principles, with facilities such as greenhouses, grow towers, and hydroponic and aquaponic ponds. These growing techniques are discussed in further detail in Chapter 5. Food production within the support district is in addition to production activities in the compounds and blocks; 70 acres is a sufficient size for self-sufficiency to feed the population of a walking shed. Nevertheless, the balance will depend on the variables of soil and climate. Despite these variables, it is important to understand the potential production that can be achieved by nesting. To demonstrate this, Paul Crabtree has produced a more thorough analysis of possible production capacities, provided in Table 3.1.

Table 3.1 Utility Infrastructure Quantities per Compound, Block, Quadrant, and Village (table prepared by Paul Crabtree)

	POPULATION	PHOTOVOLTAICS		LEACH FIELD	WATER USE
		ON ROOF	SOLAR FARM		PER DWELLING UNIT
Compound	15	2,400 s.f.	1,200 s.f.	3,000 s.f.	1,200 GPD
Block	120	19.200 s.f.	9,600 s.f.	24,000 s.f.	9,600 GPD
Quadrant	1,250	153,600 s.f.	76,800 s.f.	192,000 s.f.	76,800 GPD
Village	5,000	614,400 s.f.	585,800 s.f.	1,000,000 s.f.	400,000 GPD

Notes:
1. This chart assumes a need for 600 s.f. of photovoltaic panel surface per dwelling unit, providing 30 kWh per day.
2. This chart assumes 200 gallon per day (GDP) of water usage per dwelling unit, and 2.5 persons per household.

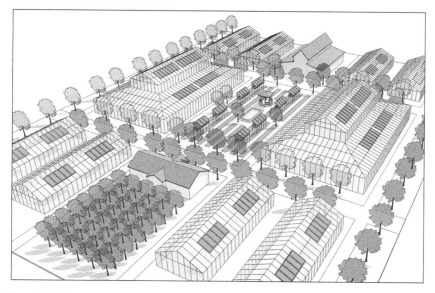

Figure 3.17 A bird's-eye view of the growing facilities. The site is arranged as a civic park open to visitors. Greenhouses, grow towers, orchards, growing plots, a farm building and a general storage and support building are among the possible facilities.

The support districts, especially the food farm, need to be treated as civic places for residents to participate in and enjoy. Figures 3.17 and 3.18 provide a site arrangement where greenhouses are placed around gardens functioning as civic parks. A barn and support building may be included. The possible coexistence of food growing, energy production facilities, and civic participation contribute to these shared activities.

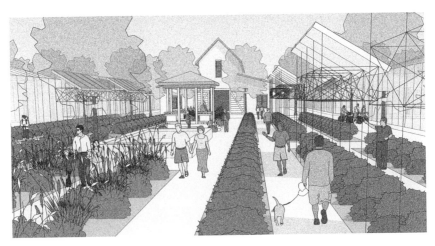

Figure 3.18 An eye-level view of the plaza shown in Figure 3.17.

Areas for four waste systems are shown on the plan in Figure 3.2. Each of these serves a quadrant and a quarter of the village center, for a population of approximately 1250. These are localized recycling and waste systems, including leach fields or similar waste processing facilities. Each field occupies approximately 8 acres, all four totaling 32 acres, which is actually greater than the minimum required amount shown in Table 3.1.

The Circulation Network

The circulation network connects all the parts of the village with safe, efficient, and pleasurable thoroughfares accommodating all modes of transportation, but principally walking (Figures 3.19 and 3.20). The design of this network follows two principles. The first is slow speed; there is no need for high-speed roads in a settlement that operates primarily within a walking shed. The second is sharing; pedestrians may easily share these thoroughfares with low-speed motorized and non-motorized vehicles, with no separation or sidewalks. There are sidewalks only on regular streets, which are limited to those leading to the village center and looping around the central greens. The loop accommodates on-street parking for the business row. Street trees are placed either in tree grates with wide sidewalks or on tree lawns located in between the street and detached sidewalks. The four cardinal streets connecting regionally are most probably existing streets with their speed limits reduced within the pedestrian shed. No vehicle would need to travel these streets at more than 25 miles per hour speed.

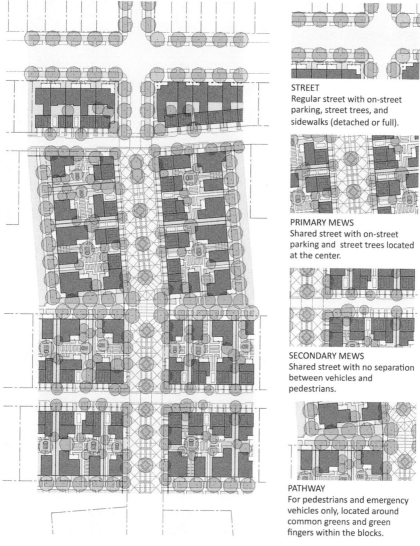

STREET
Regular street with on-street
parking, street trees, and
sidewalks (detached or full).

PRIMARY MEWS
Shared street with on-street
parking and street trees located
at the center.

SECONDARY MEWS
Shared street with no separation
between vehicles and
pedestrians.

PATHWAY
For pedestrians and emergency
vehicles only, located around
common greens and green
fingers within the blocks.

Figure 3.19 A detailed plan segment illustrating the thoroughfare types in context. On the right is a key that identifies each of the four thoroughfare types employed within the adaptation village.

Mews and pathways form the rest of the thoroughfare network. The primary mews, which form the loop that goes around the first ring of blocks (as shown by wider gray on the plan in Figure 3.2), accommodate trees and on-street parking at the center of the thoroughfare. The suggested right-of-way width is 60 feet. The secondary mews are narrow, like alleys, but designed to accommodate a higher level of conviviality. They simultaneously support

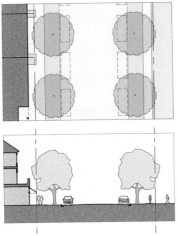

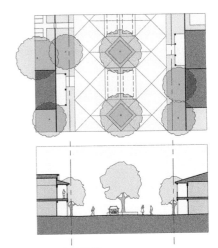

STREET
Regular street with on-street parking, street trees, and sidewalks (detached or full).
Right of way: Varies between 60 to 80 feet
Curb-to-curb dimension: Varies between 32 to 44 feet

PRIMARY MEWS
Shared street with on-street parking and street trees located at the center.
(Right of way: 60 feet recommended
Pavement width: Varies with minimum 20 feet clearance

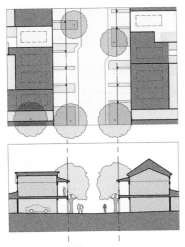

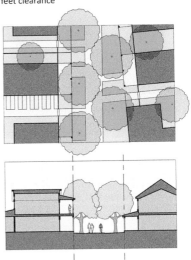

SECONDARY MEWS
Shared street with no separation between vehicles and pedestrians.
Right of way: 30 feet recommended
Pavement width: Varies with minimum 20 feet clearance

PATHWAY
For pedestrians and emergency vehicles only, located around common greens and green fingers within the blocks.
Right of way: varies around 40 feet
Pavement width: 5 or 10 feet

Figure 3.20 Partial plans and cross sections of four thoroughfare types employed within the adaptation village.

Figure 3.21 An eye-level view of a secondary mews.

neighborly interaction, front the occasional businesses within the compounds, and provide vehicular access. The suggested right-of-way width is 30 feet. Mews are shared thoroughfares; there are no curbs separating pedestrians from vehicles. Changes in pavement as well as shifts in alignment calm the traffic and encourage pedestrian use. They have no fancy front yards; they are expedient and modest. The life on the mews is richer and more inclusive in social engagement and productivity than the streets (Figure 3.21).

The smallest thoroughfares are the pathways that go through the blocks, forming a fine-grained network of pedestrian circulation. They provide a pleasant walking experience with many opportunities for social interaction. Two of the pathways on each block are wider to accommodate occasional emergency and service vehicles (as shown on the plan in Figure 3.7).

Notes

1   The workshop took place in the office of Pel-Ona Architects and Urbanists in Boulder, Colorado, between February 13 and 15, 2020. The assumed location for the adaptation village was close to Erie, Colorado, a half-hour drive north of Denver. The participants in this 3-day workshop were Andrés Duany, Korkut Onaran, Peter Swift, Ronnie Pelusio, Alexander Person III, Ryan Handy, Alex Hemmer, Melissa Harrison, Matt Johnson, Daniel Sailor, and Caresa Atencio. The workshop was finalized with a presentation Andrés and Korkut provided at the University of Colorado Boulder, on February 15, 2020.
2   For further discussion, see Duany and Steutville's article titled "Defining the 15-minute city" (2021).
3   Hybrid, a term introduced by Elizabeth Plater-Zyberk, refers to multiple land uses that support each other. As opposed to the term mixed-use, where each use can function independently, the term hybrid suggests a higher level of mutual support between the uses, such as, for instance, the traditional medieval shop where the owner lives above or behind the shop.

4

ENABLING RELOCATION

Moving away from trouble is inevitable and difficult enough. It will only add to the rolling disaster if the effort is disorganized. To avoid this, a new generation of land use planning at local scales needs to be enabled. In order for this effort to be widespread and fast, there needs to be a new initiative at the federal and state levels to initiate comprehensive plans aiming at adaptation, localization, and relocation. This is the most effective way to provide for a just, orderly, and economically sustainable transition to designated "receiving zones," where more resilient lifestyles are offered. The previous chapter presented the physical characteristics of a model for building such communities within receiving zones: the adaptation village. This chapter offers policies that can make moving into the receiving zones attractive. It presents a road map for preparation of a new generation of comprehensive plans and offers policy priorities. It focuses on four policies: productive ownership, preferential tax for business, tax deduction for rent, and subsidies for localized infrastructure. Once living in the receiving zones is seen to be desirable, a new market will emerge which will guide the private sector's participation.

Why Plan for Relocation?

In the face of repeated, intensifying storms, floods, fires, landslides, and heat waves, moving away from danger is not only the most rational option, but also the most socially responsible action. Furthermore, it has been a part of

 DOI: 10.4324/9781003182627-4

American cultural history. If government is not proactive, the damage of climate disasters will exponentially waste our limited resources. Worldwide experience has taught us that uncontrolled migration occurs at times of acute crises, resulting in further unnecessary harm. It is the responsibility of political leaders, regulators, planners, and residents themselves to enable preemptive relocation to safer places in a way that results in more, not less, resilience. The alternative is the forced displacement, disorderly evacuations, rushed temporary settlements, and even social chaos that usually follow major disasters. In addition, it is likely that we will experience disruptions in supplies of food and essential goods that depend on high levels of travel, beyond the shortages of food and other supplies in disaster zones. These prospects have been discussed in Chapter 2.

Creating pockets of self-sufficiencies in the relatively safe receiving zones is the primary objective of adaptation-oriented land use planning. Receiving zones need to be established in many places on the continuum from rural to urban. As discussed in the previous chapter, these can range from new towns to the retrofitting of suburban land or infill developments, especially within partly abandoned or underused urban areas. These zones may be established across entire regions as well as on a smaller scale within a region. The move doesn't always need to be from one region to another; after all, there may be relatively safer areas even within any given 10 × 10-mile area.

The New Generation of Planning and Design

Preparing and adopting comprehensive plans that establish receiving zones are important steps towards planning for resilient prospects within these zones and enabling relocation. Even though there are no reasons why local governments (cities, counties, regional councils of governments) cannot start designating receiving zones in their comprehensive plans as described here, a push from higher-level governments (state and federal) is needed to initiate and accelerate a more widespread, comprehensive movement. The localization of zoning initiated by the Standard State Zoning Enabling Act (1924) and the Standard City Planning Enabling Act of 1928 provides the template. These Acts initiated a strong, comprehensive local planning culture in a limited time across most of the country. This is the kind of reform and initiation we need now.

The Standard City Planning Enabling Act (1928) advised preparation of *municipal plans* (first-generation comprehensive plans) and establishing *planning commissions* to provide expertise. Many urban planners are aware of this history. However, the less well-known fact about the Act is that it also provided the framework for the establishment of *regional planning commissions* to prepare *regional plans*. Section 29 of the Act reads:

> The regional planning commission, after adopting the regional plan, shall certify a copy thereof to the governor, to the planning commission of each municipality within the region, to the council of each municipality not having a planning commission, to the county commissioners of each county wholly or partly included in the region, and to other organized taxing districts or political subdivisions wholly or partly included in the region.

As for the legal status of the regional plan, Section 31 states:

> After the adoption of the regional plan by the regional planning commission, no street, no park or public way, ground or open space, no public building or other public structure, and no public utility, whether publicly or privately owned or operated, shall be constructed or authorized in nonmunicipal territory within the region until the location, character, and extent thereof shall have been submitted to and approved by the regional planning commission of the region.

The authority of the regional plan is limited to "nonmunicipal territory" as the Act also enabled municipal plans (also known as comprehensive plans) in coordination with the regional plans. The Act intended to coordinate regional and municipal authorities.

Today, a similar spirit of reform to what these Acts demonstrated in the past is badly needed to enable adaptation. This point in history calls for a renewed partnership between municipalities, especially within metropolitan areas and counties, in order to prepare a new generation of comprehensive plans to address the prospects and plan for adaptation.

Even though intergovernmental coordination hasn't been a common characteristic of planning culture everywhere within the United States, there are nevertheless many current examples. The establishment of receiving zones in the new-generation adaptation-oriented comprehensive plans can be prepared regionally by intergovernmental alliances, where such alliances are already functioning. They can be prepared at the metropolitan scale, where municipalities are already working together. They can be prepared at the county level, where municipalities are already cooperating with the county in preparing comprehensive plans. They can also be prepared by new intergovernmental partnerships.

Start with Mapping

The first step is creating receiving zones, with mapping at all practical scales. The technical data are available. Mapping needs to be based on (a) the long-term risks of climate-related events such as storms, floods, fires, landslides, and heat waves; (b) non-climate-related risks such as earthquakes and volcanoes; (c) availability of water, sun, and fertile soil; and (d) current health risks due to air, water, and soil pollution.[1] These *risk and opportunity maps* may be commissioned by the states and prepared by consultants or universities. Once issued by the state, the maps would invite alliances of municipalities and counties to prepare adaptation models for their comprehensive plans. The plans would indicate receiving areas and, where politically feasible, high-risk areas. Before adoption, the state would review the plans. Depending on the political situation, the state may mandate or suggest revisions in these boundaries. The last step would be local: the local municipalities, alliances, or counties would adopt their comprehensive plans.

Commitment to Adaptation Policies

For receiving zones to increase resilience and create an environment where life can endure better in spite of future disruptions, the comprehensive plans need to show strong commitment to certain adaptation policies, including localization of sustenance systems within the receiving areas. Only by such commitment will a receiving zone attract those currently living in places of repeated disasters and convince them to relocate, even when it means making a difficult financial decision. As stated earlier, the objective is enabling relocation without any mandate but by making it an attractive option. A new real estate market will then emerge, and mortgage and insurance policies will further support relocation. A safer place would be reflected in the premiums.

Basic Attributes and Strategies

To enable relocation to be a financially and socially resilient option, some basic tools should be in place. As mentioned in the previous chapter, balanced localization in the walking shed is an ambitious, but nevertheless necessary, objective. High levels of self-sufficiency (especially in sustenance systems and infrastructure) need to be required within receiving zones. Self-sufficiency, however, does not necessarily mean rejecting interaction with larger-scale networks; as mentioned earlier, it means not depending on them. The local systems will be ready to sustain life when the regional systems collapse, to the degree that they were localized. There are many advantages to the walking shed being nested within biking and driving sheds, especially in existing large metropolitan areas. As stated earlier, providing most human needs and desires at biking and driving shed scale still needs to be within our vocabulary of increasing resilience.

In terms of the settlement characteristics, the Adaption Village model provides guidance. However, the creation of receiving zones offers a unique opportunity to adopt certain principles and policies that may be essential in enabling adaptation. Four of these are offered below.

Productive Ownership

Our current zoning system focuses on protecting single-family homes from disturbance by other uses via the creation of large tracts of residential use, with no other productive activity. As a result, today's residential property is often a liability for the owners: an overextended debt with no way to generate additional income. This makes households vulnerable financially. The foreclosures of 2009 gave us an idea of the financial vulnerability of the single-family house model.

It is insightful to compare the single-family house located within a single-use neighborhood with the pioneer homestead of the late 19th century. A homestead farm was almost self-sufficient. The pioneer homestead accommodated a diverse set of productive activities that were mutually supportive of each other. Crops to feed the household were essential. Goods supplied from outside were limited. It was a difficult way of life, for sure, but the fact remains that self-sufficiency is (a) possible and (b) resilient. Today, at the other end of the spectrum, we are in a position of dependency, with no productive activity permitted on the typical residential lot in a single-family residential zoning district. It is time to reverse this trend and create financial resilience for the average household. Receiving zones provide this opportunity.

Financial resilience at the lot scale can be approached in three ways: (a) in addition to residential use, permitting uses such as "cottage industry and retail" and "cottage farming" (use categories that are defined in Appendix A:

Tools for Coding); (b) encouraging rental spaces and units; and (c) enabling development to take place incrementally. A reformed version of zoning would enable a household to engage in productive activity. It has been a surprise to see how many people ran businesses from home during the isolation imposed by the COVID-19 pandemic. Permitting flexibility is the first step. Also needed are the organizational structures that encourage and enable households to engage in such productive activities. A homeowners' association (HOA), for example, may provide technical support for small-scale food growing. Such strategies are discussed in detail in Chapter 6.

The compound, which was introduced in the previous chapter, is a model that enables productive ownership by accommodating all three ways mentioned above: as conceived in the adaptation village, the compound allows the lot to accommodate productive activities, it enables the owner to rent some of the structures for income, and it provides incremental growth of finances for the long term, as the structures can be constructed incrementally over time. The compound model has been common for farms and other multipurpose cohabitation forms throughout the history of human settlements. Most compounds implied a level self-sufficiency.

Contrast the possibilities of the compound with today's typical large suburban house (a McMansion). It is a three-story house built by a developer and bought by a family who needs to pay for, and take care of, all of the floor area starting on day 1 (sizes such as 3,000–4,000 square feet are not uncommon). Years later, the kids might need to live with their spouses in the same house, as they cannot afford yet to buy a McMansion of their own. But grandma has moved out and now lives, isolated, in an expensive facility. Recently, this has become a common pattern in many suburban districts. Even though the demand for smaller units located close to services is increasing all around the United States, the supply still consists predominantly of large houses located in single-use suburban neighborhoods.[2] This makes very little sense on a social, economic, or ecological level.

In the compound alternative, the lot is permitted to accommodate almost the same amount of floor area in up to five or six structures, either residential or for work. Here is a possible scenario: a family builds a modest house of 1400 square feet to live in. They then build a 600-square-feet "granny unit." This way, instead of locking a major part of its finances into a large house, the family invests its now freed money in other opportunities. The family then continues adding buildings, one at a time as its finances permit, for rent or for married kids to move into. Rental spaces then give an affordable living option for formation of other families, as well as encouraging social interaction and cooperation. The possibilities are many. Enabling the compound model generates gradually increasing income for the household on the same size of lot with the same amount of building area, as opposed to building a financial burden. In conclusion, compound model needs to be adopted as one of the primary lot types by the zoning ordinances for communities within the receiving zones. More details about regulatory tools are provided in Appendix A: Tools for Coding.

Preferential Tax for Business

Creating a strong local economy by means of a diverse group of businesses is essential for achieving self-sufficiency within the walking sheds in receiving zones. Preferential tax treatment for businesses is a policy to encourage development in these zones. This tool has been used successfully to spur economic development and job creation in distressed communities. The opportunity zones initiated by the Tax Cuts and Jobs Act of 2017 are part of a strong preferential tax program that has helped many communities recently, and it can be extended to receiving zones by nomination by the Secretary of the U.S. Treasury.[3]

Preferential tax policies are needed for the walking shed to accommodate production of certain essential goods to increase self-sufficiency, and this is difficult if we depend only on the market. In addition to encouraging some small businesses and start-ups, a preferential tax treatment program such as established opportunity zones is an effective way to encourage a strong entrepreneurial business environment in receiving zones. Furthermore, extended tax credits to small businesses moving from a high-risk zone would encourage and enable the move. This support can be justified because it serves the public purpose as a more resilient lifestyle is a responsible and proactive response to climate crisis.

Tax Deduction for Rent

In the U.S., home ownership is favored over renting by many policies, including a tax system that allows mortgage interest to be deducted. Yet, ownership does not suggest an attractive lifestyle for everyone. Renting is an alternative for young singles and young families, for whom ownership is not yet possible. Renting can also be an attractive option for empty nesters and people who are considering relocation. Renting encourages and enables mobility. Furthermore, ownership usually drains the finances of young households with limited financial means and takes away their ability to make alternative investments. Receiving zones must necessarily accommodate both people who rent and people who own. However, in order to achieve this, policies such as tax deduction for rent need to be adopted so that renting becomes a financially attractive option too.

Another important factor that can make renting an attractive option concerns the location and quality of rental units. Rental units need to be different than the commonplace apartment monoculture – isolated apartmentvilles surrounded by parking lots, located at the edges of cities and neighborhoods, and distanced from other residential prototypes, which removes the possibility of any self-sufficiency and synergistic relationships between lifestyles. This is the opposite of what diversity and resilience require. Developments within receiving zones need to mix people who rent with people who own in close proximity so that they can support each other. The blended compound model accommodates this. Within the self-sufficient walking shed, rental places need to be offered nearby for the workers of the businesses, which is essential in creating a diverse local economy. Renting needs to be an attractive option also for people who are relocating with limited financial means. It becomes so when it offers affordable living that is close to local jobs.

Tax deductions for mortgage interest have encouraged ownership and relocation to the suburbs. Today, tax deductions for rent can encourage moves to receiving zones, especially if they make renting a financially rational option. With tax deduction for rent, part of residents' wealth can be productive in other endeavors. There need to be two prerequisites for tax deduction for rent: (1) the primary bread-winning work for the household must be within the walking or biking shed, and (2) the rental unit must be located on the same lot where the owner/landlord lives.[4]

A targeted tax policy will increase important aspects of adaptation, such as the move to a receiving zone and socioeconomic diversity within the walking shed. This is a market that would not otherwise come into being in time for the consequences of the climate disaster and thus has both public as well as private benefits.

Subsidies for Localized Infrastructure

There is not enough money to repeatedly rebuild in risk areas each time a disaster happens.[5] FEMA sources will likely ensue, but the disaster help and hazard mitigation focus needs to shift from rebuilding towards financing localized infrastructure within receiving zones. Funds are better used to subsidize localized infrastructure within receiving zones as a part of protecting citizens from future disasters. This should be within the scope of FEMA; only the form is different – it is proactive support rather than reactive. Within this framework, help may come from the Hazard Mitigation Grant Program (controlled by states), HUD Community Development Block Grants, and Homeland Security's Infrastructure Security Program.[6]

If targeted well, government subsidies are helpful in changing local trends fast. Localizing the infrastructure is an effective target for creating resilient communities of the future. However, this doesn't mean that change cannot happen without the subsidies. As will be summarized in the next chapter, technologies to localize sustenance systems are available. We need to comprehend the necessity for them and act now.

Notes

1 This list was inspired by a presentation provided by Scott Bernstein at the California Adaptation Forum organized by CNU California in March 2020. See also the work of the Center for Neighborhood Technology at www.cnt.org
2 For a well-documented analysis of the recent and projected housing supply and demands in the U.S., see *Reshaping Metropolitan America: Development trends and opportunities to 2030* by Arthur C. Nelson (2013). Also see Nelson (2020).
3 For more information about opportunity zones, please visit www.irs.gov/credits-deductions/opportunity-zones-frequently-asked-questions. See also Din (2018).
4 For further discussion on subsidies for rental housing please see articles by Brueckner (2014) and DiPasquale (2011). Also, there are insightful arguments within the book by Schwartz et al. (2016).
5 For a financial history of rebuilding on the barrier islands on the East Coast of the United States, see the book *Geography of Risk* by Gaul (2019).
6 The list of possible funding sources was provided by Laura Clemons of Collaborative Communities, in a private conversation.

5

LOCALIZING SUSTENANCE SYSTEMS

What do we need to sustain life? We need to produce energy and food; we need to store and distribute water; we need a way to handle our waste; and we need a means of producing essential goods that we use daily, such as tools and clothing. Localization of these sustenance systems is a crucial step in creating pockets of self-sufficiencies and thus enabling adaptation. In this chapter, we will review strategies as well as available technologies that can initiate and establish successful localization.

General Strategies

Two of the concepts listed in the "governance" and "design principles" columns in Table 1.1 have implications for localization of sustenance systems as well. These are nesting and subsidiarity.

Nesting refers to creating a hierarchy of units that can fit within each other. A building nested within a compound shares various amenities of the compound. A compound nests within a block, where additional facilities are shared at the block scale. A block nests within a quadrant, and a quadrant within a walking shed, with common amenities that are appropriate to share at the quadrant and walking shed scales. A walking shed nests within a city or a region. Subsidiarity is a principle of governance that refers to making decisions at the most local level that is possible, practical, and effective. If a decision can be made at a lower level, the higher governance unit should cede the right to do so. Subsidiarity, combined with nesting, enables us to

DOI: 10.4324/9781003182627-5

establish and govern sustenance systems at various scales. We can produce energy, store water, and grow food not just at household and regional scales, as is usually the case, but also at compound, block, quadrant, and walking shed scales. Taking water as an example, currently, municipal or regional networks are the primary providers of water to most of our communities. We need to construct water storage at smaller scales. A single building or a compound may have a modest cistern. A water well and a water tower may meet the needs of a block to a significant degree. Larger cisterns and water storage may serve the walking shed. These facilities may reduce our dependence on citywide and regional water networks. The stronger the supplies within smaller local units, the more self-sufficient they become. This is how supplies and production at various scales, nesting within each other, create a more resilient lifestyle. Improvements can be implemented and function in an incremental way. This is the strength of localization.

Technology

The argument for rejecting high-tech and focusing on low-tech: although humans did fine without advanced technology for centuries, today it is hard to imagine a life without, for example, computers, smartphones, and other "high-tech" devices. Despite our utter dependency, most of us don't know how these gadgets work or how they can be repaired. The design and the production of many of these tools are monopolized by a few companies that function in the market at a global scale. In contrast, tools of the past provided more autonomy and resilience to a household. Farmstead farmers, for instance, not too long ago, knew how windmills powered the water pumps that brought up the water from the wells, how the reapers and plows worked the land, how spinning wheels and looms produced fabric for clothing, and so on. Tools were simple to understand, and it was possible to repair most on the premises. Faced with these observations, it is easy to argue that self-sufficiency of sustenance systems, especially at the scale of the household, compound, and block, necessitates bringing back simple and modest technologies of the past, because they provided autonomy and independence. Dependence on the advanced technological gadgets that are controlled by distant global companies makes us vulnerable.

The counter-argument for not rejecting high-tech but for localizing it: although localization of sustenance systems requires tools that are not made, assembled, and distributed via global networks, this is not enough reason to reject advanced technology. Rather, we need to focus on local-izing it. There are many exemplary efforts – in the United States and in other parts of the globe – of local control and ownership of advanced technologies, including semi-independent internet mesh networks,[1] inde-pendent electrical power systems,[2] and production of advanced devices by local means.[3] The idea of localizing advanced technology is a paradigm shift in the way we approach engineering. But it needs to happen; engi-neering needs to innovate and enable local technology in order to achieve and sustain self-sufficient communities. This is not a matter of choice but a matter of survival.

In the meantime, an encouraging number of technologies and strategies that can enable localization of sustenance systems do already exist. These are reviewed in the rest of this chapter.

Energy

Solar, wind, hydro-, biomass, and geothermal power offer clean energy and can do so at the household, compound, block, and walking shed scales. The principles of nesting and subsidiarity hold the key.

Solar panels at the building scale to provide hot water have long been a common technology in many parts of the world. Photovoltaic panels are becoming an ever more reliable source of electricity. Net metering allows households to feed the grid and other households when surplus energy is produced. The network then credits the subscriber for future use. Unfortu-nately, utility companies do not allow energy production by subscribers to be independent, even for limited periods of time. Households do not have a cut-off switch; if the grid goes down, so does the power for the subscribers. This is the case even if they can produce enough energy for themselves with their solar panels. This restriction is not a matter of technology but policy; the underlying issue is that households as independent producers threaten the hegemony of the power companies.[4]

Certain states have already adopted legislation aiming at initiating local-ization of their energy systems, with Hawaii leading the way.[5] There are also some recent communities with microgrids, in which a neighborhood provides its own power while still connected to the utilities' grid, but they are the exception. Currently, in the majority of regions, the household and the regional network are the only scales where almost all energy production happens. This leaves us vulnerable to brownouts.[6] We need to revisit our energy policies and invest in energy production at compound, block, and neighborhood scales. The quantity of electricity that can be produced at the compound, block, and neighborhood scales (by rooftop solar panels, small wind turbines such as 30-foot-tall towers, geothermal, micro-hydro, or biogas as components of a microgrid) can significantly support overall energy production. Even a solar-powered garden light fixture has a place within the hierarchy of energy production. Energy production at block and neighborhood scales will be especially needed by the essential businesses in a village or a neighborhood center, so that they can continue to function in regional emergencies. Microgrids at the scale of the walking shed can achieve surprising efficiencies with new technologies such as concentrating solar power (CSP) mirrors. And, within the range of a 15-minute driving shed, there may even be an opportunity for a methane-powered power plant at a landfill site, or a hydro-powered dam, or even a micro-nuclear plant.[7] Each of these localized systems must continue functioning independently if and when the regional power goes down, as usually occurs in disaster zones. This enables resilience and self-sufficiency at the scale of the walking shed. At the quadrant and walking shed scales, biodigesters, waste incineration systems, geothermal heat pumps, and micro-hydro turbines (where creeks and rivers are available) can also supplement the other systems.[8] Shared batteries and generators at the scale of the compound and block may be helpful in dealing with short-term emergencies.

Production is one side of the equation. Consumption is the other. In daily life, finding ways to reduce energy consumption increases resilience. Energy-efficient appliances, lights, and temperature-control systems are a good start. However, when it comes to physical environments that respond to climatic conditions, previous generations did a much better job. When mechanical heating and cooling and advanced insulation options were not available, we relied on cross ventilation, protected courtyards, breezeways, wind towers, and tree canopies for cooling. In cold regions, we created compact buildings with walls of high thermal mass to maximize passive solar gain. We had fireplaces and stoves that heated not only the air but also the walls of a building to maximize long-term heat retention. We need to relearn how to build without depending on heavy energy consumption for cooling and heating. Climate-conscious design is one of the design principles that we discuss in Chapter 7, where we will review building types that evolved through generations of learning how to respond to the climatic conditions and create comfort zones naturally, without the use of advanced machinery that consumes energy.

Water

Water supplies share vulnerability with energy production systems and thus also share some resilience strategies. Lessening the amount of water that we use and securing water storage go hand in hand. In urban areas, regional networks are usually a household's only source of water. Households are completely vulnerable to water shortages or pollution at the source. Here, again, nesting of sources and storage is the key to resilience, through localized support at the compound, block, quadrant, and walking shed scales. Fortunately, water can be supplied at these scales by modest means, such as rainwater harvesting, cisterns, wells, and water towers.

At the household and compound scales, cisterns that capture rain from roofs have been one of the most reliable water sources throughout history. They can provide a significant portion of the water needed in many locations around the nation. Yet they are not usually a part of recent development models – one of the many vulnerabilities created by large-network water distribution systems, supposedly in the name of efficiency. Rainwater capture is actually regulated in some regions, such as in Colorado, where the permitted amount that can be captured in cisterns is limited.[9] Some of these outdated water laws must and will be reformed, as we become more and more aware of the fact that self-sufficiency will be a matter of survival.

At the block and walking shed scales, wells and cisterns fed by impervious surfaces may supply the need significantly, with limited dependence on an outside supply. Larger cisterns and reservoirs at walking shed scale may be needed, depending on the climate. Cisterns located underneath community buildings or plazas have been common in many settlements in the past. The historic *Bottini* of Siena,[10] cisterns in Alcàzar Palace, Seville (Figure 5.1), and cisterns in Constantinople (Figure 5.2) are three impressive examples that supplied the water needs of entire communities. Implementing and running these kinds of facilities necessitate local competence, to be discussed in detail in the next chapter.

As with energy, reducing water consumption is also a significant step on the path to resilience. Common methods include installing low-flow fixtures, xeriscaping, use of gray water for irrigation, and gardens with well-designed swales. We will never achieve self-sufficiency if we continue watering our

Figure 5.1 Cisterns under Alcàzar Palace, Seville.

Figure 5.2 Cisterns under the old town of Constantinople, modern İstanbul.

front lawns and golf courses in regions with an especially hot, arid climate: watering priority should be for food production and for providing comfort zones by means of plant material that can prevent formation of heat islands. In the support districts, integrating agriculture should consider the Yeomans keyline plan (Yeomans 1981; see also Yeoman 1993). This is a low-tech permaculture system and structure for a settlement layout based on the topography of the specific site. It enhances utilization of rainfall, builds soil, provides for livestock and crops, enhances forests, and reduces wildfire hazards. This brings us to our next subject: food.

Food

Food, and our relationship with it, has reached a sorry state. Increasing food production per unit of labor as the primary objective has led to the mechanization and homogenization of agriculture and created a landscape of monoculture: acres and acres of corn, soybean, or wheat fields managed by large industrial agriculture businesses. This has cost us dearly. We are using more water for irrigation owing to the scale of the systems and evaporation. We are using herbicides, pesticides, and fertilizers that sustain large monocultures but weaken the soil and compromise water quality. Produce is bred to withstand shipping and freezing at the expense of nutritional quality. Today, there are so-called "food deserts" not only in the inner cities, but in rural counties as well; there is hunger in the middle of farming country, especially in the West and Midwest. This level of industrialized agriculture can continue only with government subsidies. Food that could be grown right next door is instead transported hundreds and even thousands of miles, which is a significant waste of energy. The increasing distance between production and consumption alienates us from what we eat and how it is produced. It makes us dependent on the industrial agriculture system, even though growing food was an integral part of our daily culture not too long ago. Today, there are farmers who cannot feed their families. As the local knowledge and culture of food production diminish, life becomes more and more vulnerable.[11] The good news is that there are also strong initiatives to localize food production and regain and reclaim a local food culture, even in urban locations.

When localization of food production is mentioned, the amount of land is often a question that is asked: how many acres do we need to feed a certain population? As noted above, for the adaptation village model, we recommend a population density of 18 people per acre. This density accommodates a population of around 5,000 within the walking shed. According to some food indices, this would require at least an additional 5,000 acres of land.[12] However, these indices are flawed for three reasons. First, they assume mechanized and monoculture agriculture, not the next generation of localized, diverse food growing techniques and cultures we are about to review. Second, the calculations are bloated by including the amount of land needed to conventionally grow the food to feed livestock. Third, they omit local production within the community (also known as urban agriculture), where food is grown in private yards, community gardens, and other community food growing centers. Modest gardens do supply families and restaurants significantly. In some new developments, instead of the typical club house or golf course, HOAs are investing in a cooperative farm to encourage gardening and food production. In some jurisdictions today, zoning accommodates poultry, rabbits, and even miniature goats (for their milk) within residential zone districts.

There are many exemplary efforts producing food locally and sustainably using the concept of crop diversity. These aim at producing an ideal variety of fresh foods to feed locals, instead of maximized, monocultured crops shipped far away. Permaculture is being employed in some households, family farms, community gardens, and school gardens. The principles of permaculture, with a diverse set of activities supporting each other, allow large amounts of food to be produced cleanly, in a limited space, and without relying on heavy machinery and polluting chemicals. Compact, permaculture-based urban farms and urban greenhouses are becoming popular in many urban centers.[13] In addition to growing produce, activities such as poultry and fish raising and limited animal husbandry support each other. There are nonprofits that focus on urban greenhouses, especially in underused urban land patches, such as front yards and tree lawns.[14] Where land is limited, hydroponic and aquaponic farming can perform miracles. Hydroponic farming is a method of growing plants using mineral nutrient solutions instead of soil. Aquaponics is a form of agriculture that combines raising fish in tanks with soilless plant culture, where the nutrient-rich water from raising fish provides a natural fertilizer for the plants, while the plants help to purify the water for the fish (Figure 5.3).[15]

When food-growing practices follow permaculture principles and employ some of the above-mentioned diverse practices, it is possible to produce a

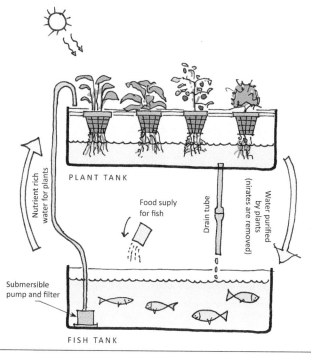

Figure 5.3 A diagram showing an aquaponics system.

large amount of nutritious food in a limited space. As mentioned before, the adaptation village assigns 70 acres for food production and 70 acres for energy production. Depending on the climate and geography of the location, these functions can be combined so that, for example, greenhouses may accommodate some solar panels. Food production in the support district, together with production at compound, block, and quadrant scales, can sufficiently feed the population of a walking shed.

Waste

There are two basic types of waste: human waste (sewage) and garbage. Local practices can help ease the impact of both.

Conventional large-scale sewage and wastewater treatment systems solve one problem while creating others. On the upside, the systems work efficiently and do take waste away from the premises, not to be seen, smelled, or worried about any longer. On the downside, the process requires that a lot of water be combined with solids to dilute them for transport. Later, somewhere else, the solids and the liquid are separated, bacteria are broken down, chemicals such as chlorine are added, and, finally, contaminants such as phosphorus and nitrogen are removed. The treated waste is then clean enough to be released into a natural body of water. Close to 80 percent of human waste in the United States is treated this way.[16] This system is itself wasteful, and soon it will no longer be practical or even possible: with the coming water shortages, even in locations with high rain averages, we will not have the luxury of using clean water to operate our conventional sewage systems.

These systems are also vulnerable to overload or failure. In severe storm events, which are becoming more frequent, the waste is released to a clean water source. This is a common problem, especially where storm water and sewage are not separated, which is the case in many municipalities.[17] According to the EPA, drinking water contamination is the result of such harmful chemicals as phosphorus and nitrogen, found in untreated sewage. Each year, there are between 23,000 and 75,000 sewage overflows. This problem will be exacerbated with the increasing frequency of unpredictable weather events.[18]

Communities within receiving zones offer a necessary opportunity for reform. At the least, new developments should not contribute to the problem. Thus, where feasible, no new development should (a) combine wastewater with storm water or (b) connect to existing municipal processing systems. These decisions will not only avoid overloading the current systems but also contribute to resilience via pockets of self-sufficiencies. Even the centralized systems can be and should be divided into smaller ones incrementally.

Smaller localized systems need to be a priority within the receiving zones. In such systems, storm water is separated from human waste at the outset, by design. Instead of treating the potable rainwater as waste, as mentioned earlier, it should be captured and utilized by cisterns, other small depositories, or bio-swales. The larger the system, the more vulnerable it is and likely to fail. Systems at household and compound scales leave less chance of catastrophe. The same holds for septic tanks, leach fields, lagoons, and constructed wetlands. Well-designed septic tanks and leach fields are also effective at replenishing the aquifer. However, household or compound scale systems may not always be the most feasible choice for higher densities. Constructed wetlands are especially efficient at walking shed scales. As mentioned in our discussion of the adaptation village, dividing the walking shed into smaller quadrants and providing each with its own system is another option. Accordingly, good soil and deep groundwater conditions need to be among the criteria for site election of any development within a receiving zone.

There is an inherent problem in mixing valuable potable water with valuable human excrement just to flush it away, only to have the problem of separating and treating the combination. This can be resolved with the proven high-low technology of composting toilets; they reduce water demand, and the "waste" becomes fertilizer for food production. This can be implemented at the block or quadrant scales.[19]

The other main form of waste is "garbage." Instead of trucking it to far-off landfill, most of it can be processed within the walking shed. Communities that created zero or almost zero garbage were common not too long ago in our history. If we invest in composting and recycling at various scales, nesting within each other, we can achieve almost zero garbage community within the walking shed. At the compound and block scales, we can compost simple organic matter such as fruit and vegetable waste. At larger scales – quadrant or walking shed scales – composting technology, such as a biodigester, rocket composter, or rotary composter, can be implemented. These composters use heat such as that generated by wood pellets to balance the fluidity and bacteria, and thus they can accept a wider range of waste. The resulting soil is a valuable contribution to the food production strategies discussed above. At a higher scale, waste incineration systems can also contribute to energy production.

Production of Essential Goods

On the path to creating a strong local business economy, in many small towns and urban centers, there are two primary, interrelated challenges. The first is "leakage" – money earned in a community is spent elsewhere. The second is "dependence" – the franchises of national chains suck business away from local shops and have limited or no commitment to contributing to the community life or hiring local employees. Today, most of the businesses in many communities are controlled by outside corporations and investment trusts. This is also the case when a large business employs a large part of the workforce (as is the case in many distribution centers). This makes communities vulnerable to fluctuations in the market and the policy changes of major businesses. Towns are deserted when such a business moves away or shuts down, even temporarily.[20]

Fluctuations in employment are only one problem. Others are the procurement of materials, the production of essential goods, and the provision of services. Towns struggle to keep essential services in the community, including dentists, doctors, technicians, shoe repairers, plumbers, carpenters, schools, lawyers, engineers, and so on, as well as essential supplies such as those found in hardware stores. It is very common for residents to travel long distances out of the community to find these materials and services elsewhere.

This situation may be only a matter of inconvenience today, not a matter of survival. But a possible future must assume that supply routes may be at least temporarily disrupted. If these essential materials, goods, and services are available locally, lives are much more sustainable. Imagine nothing more likely than transportation becoming difficult owing to a gas shortage – an increasingly likely scenario.

There are solutions. Among them are sourcing raw materials nearby, diversifying the economy by investing in small local businesses, supporting start-ups and creative initiatives via local support networks and maker spaces, and subsidizing essential services (schools and medical centers), even if they aren't moneymakers. In this we need to realize that no business is too small if it is local. These strategies support an entrepreneurial ecosystem of start-up businesses that has a ripple effect. An entrepreneurial ecosystem is similar to a natural ecosystem that supplies certain conditions for certain species to flourish. Start-ups need certain conditions, including opportunities for similar businesses to compete with or complement their services. This is the way the business landscape can be diversified, and essential services can find their niches in this environment.[21] Opportunity zones or similar preferential tax treatment programs mentioned in the previous chapter are a start.

The message of self-sufficiency, achieved with the comprehensive array of strategies proposed in this book, can itself lead to the promise of a more resilient lifestyle and attract aspiring business starters into these communities. However, there is reason to be more aggressive. For example, it is possible to establish, in each quadrant or walking shed, a computer center, a semi-independent mesh network, along with a maker place with at least one 3D printer. Examples of these models do exist.[22] It is possible for these kinds of facilities to be offered within the walking shed and a larger diversity of amenities within the 15-minute biking and driving sheds. The next chapter engages with how this can be financed and governed at various subsidiary scales.

Finally, there are two supports needed for a local entrepreneurial ecosystem: provision of affordable dwellings for the young labor force and provision of available space for businesses. Sometimes, conventional zoning alone is sufficient to push away start-ups if accommodations are overregulated; exclusionary use regulations do not create a good business environment and do not permit attainable housing options to be located in close proximity. Rules showing how commercial and manufacturing uses can be accommodated together with residential uses and encouraged, rather than being excluded from these neighborhoods, are essential. These rules are discussed in further detail in Appendix A: Tools for Coding. In terms of space, it is important to provide size options as well as opportunities to grow. We need to realize that, in order to create self-sufficient walking sheds, modest light industrial and manufacturing activities need to live together with commercial and residential activities, sometimes even on the same lot, as we have shown via the business row building prototypes in Chapter 3.

In closing, many of the strategies and technologies in this chapter support each other. They should be implemented together to be effective. It is time to create pockets of self-sufficiencies that increase resilience and enable adaptation.

Notes

1 When superstorm Sandy hit the East Coast in 2012, a local Wi-Fi infrastructure, established by Brooklyn's Red Hook Initiative, was the only communication infrastructure that kept working in the neighborhood. This local organization, formed by young residents, nonprofit workers, and some city officials, foresaw the importance of creating a semi-independent mesh network so as to achieve resiliency. (For more information about the Red Hook Initiative please visit https://rhicenter.org).
2 Localizing high-tech happens already in many parts of the globe – mostly by necessity. The lack of electrical grids throughout Africa, for instance, has inspired the formation of off-the-grid power start-up companies such as Greenlight Planet, d.light, and Off-Grid Electric, among others, who aim to enable communities to establish their own energy sources. Ramesh Srinivasan's (2019) book *Beyond the Valley: How innovators around the world are overcoming inequality and creating the technologies of tomorrow*, provides a comprehensive review of these companies and initiatives that function at a local level with limited resources. See also his previous book, *Whose Global Village? Rethinking how technology shapes our world* (2017) for further discussion of inequities created by global information technology networks and how some local initiatives create alternative technologies.
3 Smartphones and laptops assembled from recycled parts and scrap are common in many urban centers in Africa. Most telling is the story of the African Born 3D (AB3D) of Nairobi, a small start-up business that assembled a 3D printer out of recycled and

discarded electronics, which was then used to produce other essential tools in the community. For more information about AB3D, visit www.ab3d.co.ke/

4   For more information about energy grids at various scales and how nesting would work, see the report titled *Smart Grid System Report* (2009) by the United States Department of Energy (www.energy.gov/sites/prod/files/2009%20Smart%20Grid%20System%20 Report.pdf). For a convincing argument for localization of power, see also Bhatti and Danilovic's (2018) article titled "Making the World More Sustainable: Enabling localized energy generation and distribution on decentralized smart grid systems."

5   Shalanda Baker's (2021) book *Revolutionary Power* provides a good discussion about the background and the content of Hawaii's Act 100. She lists some of its shortcomings as well.

6   Baker (2021), in her above-mentioned book states: "Today, a centralized electricity system is actually more vulnerable than a decentralized system. When a major weather event occurs, the very interconnectivity of the electricity system means that vulnerabilities in one part of the system translate to the vulnerabilities elsewhere. Moreover, a system of centralized power increases the likelihood that one problem can lead to a cascade of problems elsewhere in the system. ... A dramatic example is the Northeast blackout in the summer of 2003, when a tree brushing against a sagging transmission line in Ohio led to the loss of power for fifty million people across eight states in the United States and Ontario. The blackout – the largest in North American history – also led to at least eleven deaths and cost $6 billion" (p. 96).

7   These technologies were proposed by Paul Crabtree during a private conversation.

8   Ibid.

9   The amount of water that can be stored in cisterns is restricted in Colorado by Colorado River Compact, a 1922 agreement between seven western states. For more information about these restrictions, see https://extension.colostate.edu/topic-areas/natural-resources/rainwater-collection-colorado-6-707/

10   Rainwater and natural springs from the hills surrounding Siena are channeled into the city via aqueducts and tunnels. The *bottini* – a word that references the barrel shape of the tunnels – follow the line between the porous upper level of limestone and the lower impermeable clay layer of the hill that Siena sits atop. For more information, visit www. invitationtotuscany.com/guide/italy/tuscany/siena/bottini-in-siena-italy

11   For a thorough review of the recent history of food production in industrial countries and in the United States, see Michael Pollan's (2009) book *In Defense of Food: An eater's manifesto.* For further discussion, see also *Food Inc.: A participant guide: How industrial food is making us sicker, fatter, and poorer – and what you can do about it,* edited by Karl Weber (2009). Also, especially for global trade subsidy statistics and consumption patterns, see *The Atlas of Food* by Millstone and Lang (2008). See also Schlosser (2002).

12   For an insightful discussion about these indices, please see the article titled "How to Sustainably Feed 10 Billion People by 2050, in 21 Charts" (Ranganathan et al. 2018). For further discussion, please see the report titled *The State of Food Security and Nutrition in the World 2019* (FAO, IFAD, UNICEF, WFP, and WHO 2019).

13   Just to give an example, GrowHaus, Denver, Colorado, produces and distributes an impressive amount of diverse food in a small urban parcel; see www.thegrowhaus.org

14   The literature about recent family farming and urban agriculture is extensive. Here, we suggest a few among many. See Wendell Berry's (2009) book *Bringing It to the Table: On farming and food* for an insightful discussion about family farms. Josh Volk's (2017) book *Compact Farms* is a good source for case studies. The book *Urban Agriculture: Diverse activities and benefits for city society,* edited by Pearson et al. (2010), provides a series of articles reviewing various urban food initiatives from various parts of the globe. In this context, we should mention the Slow Food movement as well, which is an ambitious global network that is helping to keep alive pockets of sustainable local food production. The literature about Slow Food is also voluminous. Let us suggest its founder Carlo

Petrini's books (2005, 2009, 2013), including *Slow Food Nation* and *Food & Freedom*. See also the books *Slow Living* (Parkins and Craig 2006), *Slow Democracy* (Clark and Teachout 2012) and *Slow Money* (Tasch 2008). Another important resource that makes the point for small-scale food producers for food security in the future is the report titled *Adapt Now*: A *global call for leadership on climate resilience (Global Commission on Adaptation 2020)*.

15 For further information and discussion about hydroponics and aquaponic gardening, see Baras (2018) and Bernstein (2011). For the concept of permaculture in general, see Whitefield (1993). Also visit the Permaculture Institute at https://permaculture.org. Also see the term "Permaculture" in Appendix B of this book.

16 The 80% information is from Evans (2015). For a thorough discussion about current wastewater systems in the United States, see also the book *The Humanure Handbook* (Jenkins 2005).

17 This is the case especially in the Northeast, Midwest, and Pacific Northwest. These are the very places that are experiencing unpredictable storms.

18 This information is also from Evans (2015). Some of the recent alarming news items include drinking water contamination in Toledo, Ohio, ocean contamination off Long Island, and the dead zone in the Gulf of Mexico. For further discussion, see Levine (2014).

19 For further discussion on local systems, see Scherer (2015) and Jenkins (2005). Chapter 3, titled "Green Small Towns," of the book *Planning Small and Mid-sized Towns: Designing and retrofitting for sustainability* (Friedman 2014) also provides a good summary of local systems.

20 For an insightful discussion about the issues on the planning agenda of a small town, please see Knox and Mayer (2013). For further discussion about leakage and economic dependence, see Moltz and McCray (2012); and, for leakage and dependence especially and touristic towns, see Chambers (2000).

21 Philip E. Auerswald's (2015) paper titled "Enabling Entrepreneurial Ecosystems" is a good resource for further discussion on the subject.

22 Start.coop (https://start.coop) and Digicoop (http://digicoop.io/en) are two examples among many. For an insightful discussion on the subject, see Walker (2018).

6

SOCIAL ORGANIZATION AND GOVERNANCE

Strong social ties provide support that is essential for achieving resilience. Isolation and distancing make us vulnerable. In the resilient communities of the future, we need the kind of ownership and governance models that not only enable residents to make decisions and manage sustenance systems effectively, but also create a social order where residents become assets for their neighbors. Who makes what decisions affecting how we live and thrive? What works best to allow and encourage the members of a community to be creative, productive, and supportive? These are essential questions for achieving a resilient lifestyle.

This chapter explores social organization principles to address these questions. It reviews models for governance and ownership at the compound, block, quadrant, and walking shed scales. These models are neither radical nor foreign; we are already familiar with versions of the organizational structures and ownership models reviewed here. But they are essential for forming resilient communities. What might be radical is (a) the amount of infrastructure and amenities to be managed at compound, block, quadrant, and walking shed scales due to the localized sustenance systems and (b) the way the management of these needs to be an integral and satisfying part of our lives.

The ownership and governance models are the "software" that is integrated into the "hardware" of the physical layout of the settlement. The models that are likely to be most resilient share certain principles that enable a society

    DOI: 10.4324/9781003182627-6

to be strong, yet agile enough for equitable adaptation. The principle of subsidiarity is the foundation for the various levels of localized management, and the prerequisites are sharing, giving, and enjoyment (Table 1.1).

Subsidiarity

The principle of subsidiarity suggests that decisions should be made at the most local level by those who are most familiar with, knowledgeable about, and competent in, the context. The central authority should perform only that which cannot be performed by local authorities, and the power to do so is ceded by the local authority to the central authority. Historically, subsidiarity has been an important organizing principle for federalism, including in the United States, where sovereignty lies with the states, and the federal government's role has been subsidiary. Currently however, the central government's role has expanded to be primary, especially in energy, transportation, and defense. It is fair to state that, today, the federal government's policies dominate most of our financial and social landscape.

However, in the realm of urban planning, the United States has experienced a rare level of decentralization, especially after the adoption of zoning by local governments via state-enabling legislation, as mentioned earlier. Today, most of the land use and infrastructure decisions are made by municipalities, counties, cities, towns, and villages. However, the kind of localization we advocate here, the kind that can create self-sufficiency at walking shed scale, needs finer levels of governance, decision-making, and management that bridge the gap between the individual household and the city hall.

There are communities where neighborhood organizations participate in land use decisions, even though these organizations do not usually own real estate, and participation is voluntary. There are also HOAs – and some are large – that function as a governance unit at a scale in between the municipality and the household. Ownership of land usually confers power at the local level. These examples address a level of governance that is missing in many other communities, but is nevertheless essential for the adaptation village. Here we suggest filling this gap at the compound, block, quadrant, and walking shed scales. Table 6.1 summarizes governance and ownership options at each of these levels.

A well-structured governance system that coincides with the physical elements of the community enables many varieties of roles and purposes. To

Table 6.1 Governance and Ownership Models

SCALE	MODELS	AMENITIES
Compound	Single ownership Condominium Lessee investment	The compound and everything on it
Block	HOA	Water well, water tower, possible wind or solar, community gardens, pocket parks
Quadrant	Master HOA branch Neighborhood organization	Quadrant Center Neighborhood park
Walking shed	Master HOA Cooperative Hybrid Municipality	Solar, wind, food farms, sewage system with leach fields, community house, maker place, parks, coop shops

work, they need to be formulated and stated clearly. This is easier when (a) the scale is more local, and (b) the level of interdependence is clear. These two conditions help residents to engage in practical interaction and keep the framework of localized sustenance systems in balance.

Governance at Compound Level

The compound is the basic unit in the adaptation village. It has a few ownership options. The first is the single ownership option: a person or a household owns the compound, lives in one of the units, and rents out the rest of the spaces; these may be dwelling units, home offices, or workshops. The second model for a compound is common ownership, that is, the condominium.[1] Cohousing as well follows the common ownership model.[2] The third option is a combination of the two, the lessee investment model, where renters, or at least some of them, become small percentage partners in the ownership and investment. This guarantees stronger commitment from those renters invested in the property and thus the long-term presence of their business if they operate one in the compound.

The single ownership model should be the predominant option as it has strong advantages: (a) it enables incremental growth or succession (a design principle that is discussed further in the next chapter); (b) it introduces rental spaces; and (c) it makes it easier to govern both the compound and the block. However, occasional condominiums or cohousing complexes may also be included to diversify lifestyle options. Occasional lessee investment models may also diversify lifestyle options, especially in compounds close to the village center, where more non-residential activity is accommodated.

The three advantages of single ownership need further exploration. Paramount among them is that it enables incremental growth or succession. Incremental growth is an important advantage. Under sole ownership, the compound allows the owner to start with a modest house. In subsequent stages, the household may accumulate wealth and build more. This not only produces income, but it also allows the owners to evaluate their social needs and proceed with the new construction accordingly. The condominium model, on the other hand, does not allow incremental growth as all must be built at once, with the owners present at the beginning. The second advantage of the single ownership model is that it introduces rental spaces of various sizes and levels of affordability. The rental option also integrates a desirable socioeconomic diversity and proximity to jobs, avoiding transportation expenses. As mentioned earlier, providing attainable housing options for the workforce is essential to create a strong local business economy within the walking shed. Finally, single ownership makes it easier to manage the compound because there is only one decision maker. It also makes it easier to manage the block, as fewer owners need to be represented in decision-making. The potential for conflict and disarray when "all are equal," which is so common in land use decisions in the U.S., is thereby reduced.

Some may claim that single ownership is undemocratic. It doesn't have to be so. Democratic decision-making should not be equated with majority rule (where there is always an unhappy minority). Democratic decision-making is the debate itself, which can be easily sustained if planned well, at the compound, block, quadrant, and walking shed levels. At the compound level, it is in the owners' interest to have renters express their preferences and participate in decision-making as they are the ones who can articulate their needs the best.

Governance at Block Level

At the block scale, pocket parks, gathering places, community gardens, and modestly scaled infrastructure elements (such as water towers, wells, solar banks, wind turbines), are among the common amenities to be managed. The simplest, easiest, and most effective ownership and management model for these amenities is the HOA, formed by the owners of the compounds.[3] Block layout matters in this regard. When the compounds are arranged around the common space in a physically well-defined and identifiable way, residents are more likely to feel empowered as a community representing their block-scale cluster. This makes management more agile in responding to the evolving needs, activities, and technologies accommodated on the block. This is the essence of the subsidiarity principle.

Even though negative experiences with HOAs are common, where for instance neighbors fight with each other over trivial issues, it is reasonable to expect that the conditions will be different when the HOA is responsible for managing certain sustenance systems such as a water well or a modest solar farm. This is when the neighbors realize that their lives depend on each other's ideas and capabilities and thus they start tolerating and seeing each other as assets. However, this necessitates a leap in faith and attitude: it requires neighbors to trust each other and engage in practical argumentation, which is only possible via the prerequisites of sharing, giving, and enjoyment, a subject discussed in the closing section of this chapter.

Governance at Quadrant and Walking Shed Levels

The HOA model works at the scale of the walking shed as well.[4] Successful examples exist in larger developments where a network of HOAs work together following the subsidiarity principle. Smaller HOAs manage the amenities within their blocks, whereas a master HOA (of which all block HOAs are members) owns and manages the common amenities at the entire community scale. In the adaptation village, these would include the parks and civic buildings located at the village center. A master HOA may also have branches to manage facilities located within the quadrant greens. Another model is to form a neighborhood association at the quadrant level. These options are not mutually exclusive; an HOA branch may work with a neighborhood organization with an appropriate division of labor and responsibilities. The master HOA may also own and manage infrastructure elements such as the solar and food farms, as well as the sewage systems with leach fields. As managing such facilities may be overwhelming for a master HOA, staff are necessary at this level. Hiring management businesses, grow house consultants, and technical service providers is also an option. This level of subsidiarity is the equivalent of a modest-scale municipality.

Another system that can be overlaid on the associations is a network of cooperatives, each focusing on a specific purpose. For instance, a food coop may run some of the grow houses. Another may run the solar farm. The cooperative model opens the door to many partnerships, with the potential of incubating local businesses. It doesn't have the clarity of governance that the HOA has. Therefore, there needs to be a balance between the business managed by the master HOA and the business to be delegated to others. Specifics of each variation will depend on the location and the social and economic context of the adaptation village. Even in a new community or neighborhood that is annexed to an existing municipality, a strong HOA is necessary to handle the localized sustenance systems. In such localities, certain services (emergency services, schools, etc.) need to be extended to the new community.

What if the receiving zone is on unincorporated county land, away from any current municipality? This is a strong possibility, considering the carrying capacities of certain regions means some unincorporated areas will be receiving zones. In most such cases, it is best to form new municipalities for the new settlements as they are not close to any existing ones.

Sharing, Giving, and Enjoyment

For any of the above-mentioned models to work effectively to create a resilient community, the residents need to be active in managing amenities and coordinating productive activities. This necessitates motivated, supportive, and creative members trusting each other and engaging in practical neighborly interaction. Sharing, giving, and enjoyment are prerequisites for achieving a social structure where these kinds of interactions are the norm.

Sharing creates interdependence and makes social interactions practical. When the systems sustaining our lives are managed by a distant city government, our motivation to get along with our neighbor diminishes, as compared with when we share some essential amenities, such as a water well or a solar bank at a block level. Sharing a car with a neighbor, for instance, forces us to be practical, reasonable, and tolerant. Tolerance is a form of giving. When we engage in managing shared amenities, we give our attention, we give our time, and, more often than not, we give our labor. If we see this as a burden instead of enjoying it, our motivation drops. Sharing, giving, and enjoyment may necessitate, for some of us, a shift in the way we organize our daily activities. We may need to decrease our dependence on a single distant job and diversify the way we make a living in order to have more flexibility and time in our daily lives. This allows us to be a part of the productive activities and management within the neighborhood.

Sharing, giving, and enjoyment are essential to achieving resilience; we need each other to face the future. We will likely not have the "luxury" of avoiding our neighbors in the near future; we may have to actually seek them out and be there for each other. The social organization principles listed in this chapter (subsidiarity, sharing, giving, and enjoyment) enable a social environment where neighbors support each other naturally. The concepts of sharing, giving, and enjoyment are explored and discussed further in Appendix B: Terms and Concepts for Adaptation Urbanism.

Notes

1 A condominium is a form of ownership where an HOA, which is a private management organization formed by all owners, owns and manages the land, and each member owns just the dwelling unit. Even though this kind of ownership is usually used for apartment buildings, where units are stacked and therefore a condominium is the only possible form of ownership, there are also examples where owners of several detached buildings decide to create a condominium and own the land collectively.

2 In cohousing developments, the developer invites the future property owners to participate in the process of identifying the building program, including the shared amenities, before construction. These shared amenities usually include meeting rooms, common dining and kitchen facilities, guest rooms, wood workshop equipment, etc. The future owners also decide about the bylaws before construction. For more information about cohousing, please refer to McCamant and Durrett (2011). Also see ScottHanson and ScottHanson (2004).

3 The HOA became widespread in the U.S., especially for the subdivisions constructed after World War II. As the name suggests, this is a private management association whose members agree, by contract, to follow established rules, the bylaws. The bylaws are usually set by the developers initially, but may be modified by the HOA once the units are occupied. There are two basic forms. In the first option, an HOA owns certain common elements, such as parks, community house, etc., but not the individual lots. The second is a condominium, where the HOA, as mentioned above, owns all the land in addition to the common elements. Each option has its advantages.

4 HOAs take various forms in mixed-use developments, and each of these may be employed in different parts of an adaptation village. One option is to form two HOAs: one for the owners of the residential units, the other for the owners of the non-residential spaces. The two HOAs work together. The other option is to form only one HOA, which is appropriate when the distinction between these uses is not sharp, as is the case in the compounds. The renters should also have a voice on matters affecting them. Creating a lessee investment program and allowing some of the renters to have shares is also an efficient way to establish an HOA of which renters who have invested are also members. This is a good way also to anchor certain essential businesses for a long term, even if they are renters.

7

DESIGN PRINCIPLES

The basic components of the adaptation village as an exemplary model have been described in Chapter 3. We have argued that this model can be implemented at diverse locations despite each location's unique design challenges. This model provides the optimum physical environment for localization of sustenance (Chapter 5), with well-defined site plan elements to accommodate the kind of social order that can enable self-sufficiency (Chapter 6). In this chapter we move onto the design principles, or DNA, of this model. These principles are nesting, transect, succession, gathering, secure place, and climate-conscious design (Table 1.1).

Nesting

Nesting is perhaps the most crucial design principle in establishing an adaptation village. As mentioned before, nesting refers to a hierarchy of groupings of graduated size that are positioned within one another. The principle works on three levels: the organization of the sustenance systems, the management of subsidiarity, and the physical environment. These are interdependent and support one another.

Nesting a smaller-scale unit within a larger-scale unit has advantages for resilience. Nested systems of energy, water, waste, and food management diminish the vulnerabilities inherent in dependence on regional and national networks. Nesting physical units coincident with the governance structures of subsidiarity allows decisions regarding organization to be governed by the

DOI: 10.4324/9781003182627-7

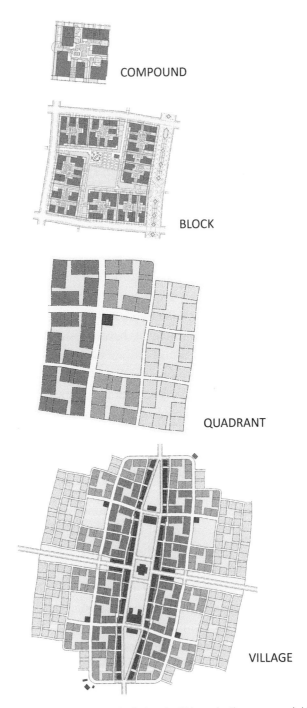

COMPOUND

BLOCK

QUADRANT

VILLAGE

Figure 7.1 Adaptation village's components that nest within each other: compound, block, quadrant, and the village.

appropriate level of local administration; this is extraordinarily important for resilience. Governance structures, as well as production systems coincident with each other, function most successfully when the physical elements of the plan are configured at each scale following the principle of nesting.

Figure 7.1 shows the plans of the components nesting within each other at various scales. The households are nested in compounds; compounds are nested within blocks; the blocks are nested within the quadrants. Finally, the quadrants come together with the village center to form the village at the walking shed scale. Each of these components is spatially well defined and easily understood in the mental maps of the residents. The geometry of the site plan will change with each settlement, but the principle for spatial organization holds.

As discussed before, an adaptation village may take the shape of a neighborhood and be implemented within an urban context. Similarly, an existing neighborhood can be repurposed as an adaptation village. Thus, nesting may continue at biking and driving sheds, that is, when the adaptation village nests within the biking and driving sheds. This is the structure of a resilient urban landscape.

To examine how governance and social organization match the nesting of the site plan components let us go back to Table 6.1, introduced in the previous chapter. The table indicates that management at the smaller scales is nested within the larger ones. The overall administration of the

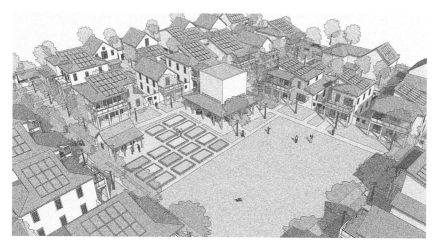

Figure 7.2 Common green, community gardens, landscaping storage shed, and water tower are among shared amenities of a typical block.

Figure 7.3 An eye-level view of the same area shown in Figure 7.2.

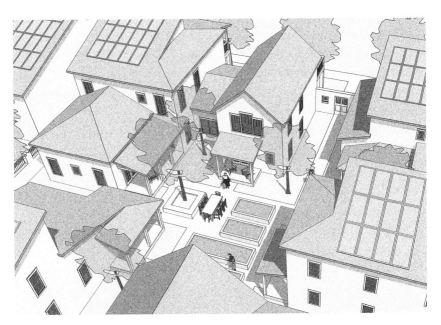

Figure 7.4 A bird's-eye view of a compound courtyard. Small courtyards, if employed and furnished well, provide a gathering place for the compound. Raised planters enable productive gardening.

settlement addresses the issues that are not best dealt with by the block, compound, and quarter administrations. The responsibilities of these bodies are associated with well-defined areas of the site plan system, thus becoming clear to participants and locally effective. The last column of the table is titled "amenities." To understand better how nesting of the amenities listed in this column matches the site plan organization, it is

Figure 7.5 An eye-level view of the same compound courtyard shown in Figure 7.4.

helpful to review the locations on the plan that accommodate two of the systems as examples: water and food. Water can be collected from rooftops and terraces in cisterns located in the compounds. The modest supply nests within the block's larger facilities, such as a well and a water tower (Figures 7.2 and 7.3). Additional water is supplied by wells in the center and from connection to the regional system – which may become sporadically unavailable. Similarly, the food production that may take place within the compound courtyards (Figures 7.4 and 7.5) nests within the block's community gardens (Figure 7.2 and 7.3). Nesting continues with the quadrant, and all this production supplements the larger-scale food production in the support district. The kind of production at higher scales is assigned depending on production in lower-scale components. This calibration can be done easily only when production levels, the organizational system, and the physical configuration follow the same nesting scheme.

Transect

A transect is a cross section that cuts through various geographical localities; it is an effective tool to compare and study these geographies. It was first introduced by field ecologists to compare a diverse set of attributes of different habitats. Transects help us understand the attributes of these habitats in a holistic way by providing a model of the complex interactions within a region.

The urban-to-rural transect, introduced by Duany Plater-Zyberk & Company, cuts through the landscape from rural to urban and explores the attributes of localities with various degrees of urbanity. It has been useful as a design instrument to establish the correlation between the many specialized components and relationships and to create contextually appropriate human environments.[1] These are immersive relationships specifying the kinds of thoroughfares, streetscapes, open spaces, building frontages, building sizes, architectural expression, landscaping, and so on. The transect reconciles the urban and the natural by providing an interrelated continuum of habitats. It allocates the preferences of human involvement in the overall environment.

Figure 7.6 shows how the urban-to-rural transect is overlaid on the adaptation village plan as the organizing principle, in concert with the principle of nesting. The village center transect zone is the most urban, densest, and most intense, with manufacturing and commercial activities. The buildings in the business row are a strong urban presence and saturated with social activity. Streetscapes as well are more urban. Open spaces are more civic in character. The three neighborhood transect zones transition to the more rural (Figure 7.7). The inner ring neighborhood transect is the densest and most urban of the three. The number of buildings, as well as the total building floor areas per compound, is the highest (see Figure 7.8, as well as Tables A1.1 and A1.2 in Appendix A: Tools for Coding). Also, the size of the compounds is more diverse within the inner ring neighborhood transect (including the full spectrum of 120 × 120 feet, 80 × 120 feet, 60 × 120 feet, and 40 × 120 feet compounds). This corresponds to the higher functional diversity, with interspersed work places including manufacturing, that is encouraged. Moving outward, the middle ring and peripheral neighborhood transect zones reduce both the number of permitted buildings and total floor area per compound. This encourages more gardening towards the peripheral locations.

The graduation in the size and type of activities across the three neighborhood transect zones is enabled by the characteristics of their built environment. The building process, while controlled within the parameters of the transect zones, should be gradual and successional in order to accommodate the changing needs of society and its economy within and outside the settlement. This ability to absorb feedback and, indeed, shocks, is the essence of resilience.

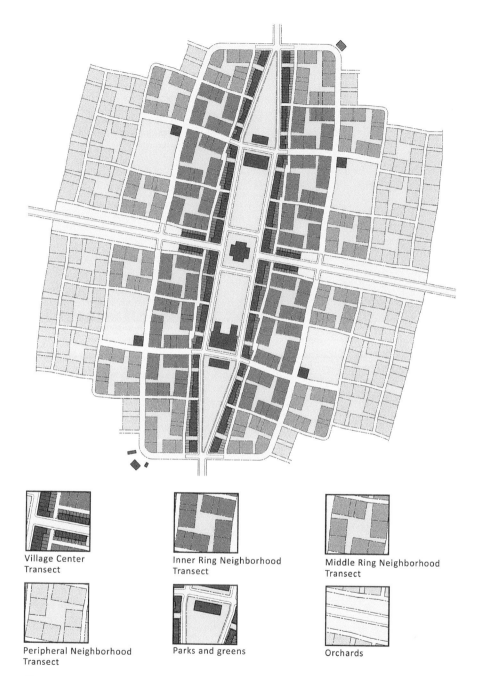

Figure 7.6 The transect plan. This plan is the regulating plan that is the basis of the form-based development code discussed in Appendix A. Under the plan is the key of all the transect zones employed within the adaptation village.

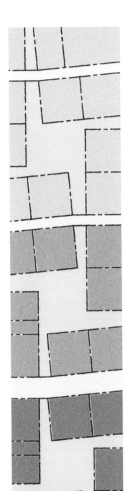

Peripheral Neighborhood Transect

- Fewer buildings in compounds
- Lower total building floor area per compound
- More gardening and cottage farming
- Less cottage industry

Middle Ring Neighborhood Transect

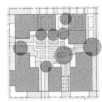

- More buildings in compounds
- Higher total building floor area per compound
- Equal amount of cottage farmingb and cottage industry

Inner Ring Neighborhood Transect

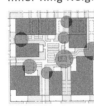

- Highest amount of buildings in compounds
- Highest total building floor area per compound
- More cottage industry
- Less cottage farming

Village Center Transect

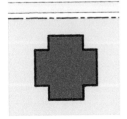
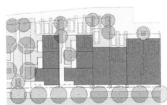

- Business row with retail, light industry and limited residential
- Civic and community buildings

Figure 7.7 The primary transect zones of the adaptation village.

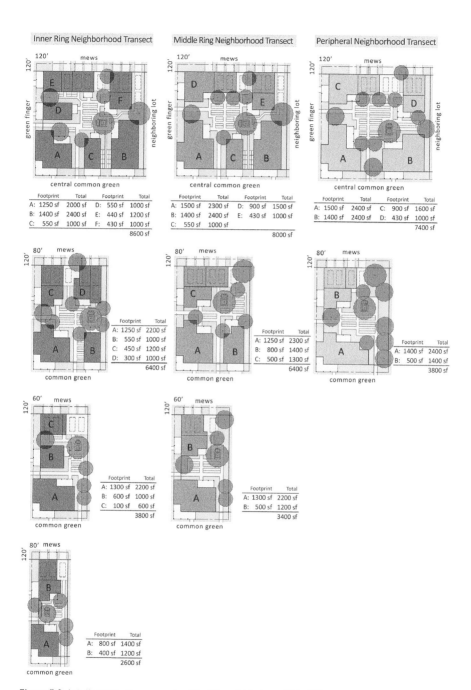

Figure 7.8 Lot diagrams of compounds with different lot sizes within different transects.

Development needs to be managed by a dynamic regulatory process with a development code that can guide such adjustments. This provides the local construction processes with the kind of agility they need to achieve resilience. The rules themselves must evolve as needed. Transect as an organizing principle provides a structure for the development code. General principles of the kind of dynamic regulation culture appropriate for the adaptation village are outlined in Appendix A: Tools for Coding. Here, let us just state that the code enforcement in the adaptation village needs to merge into the management of daily activities at local levels. In other words, the review processes need to be structured following the subsidiarity principle as well.

Succession

Succession is another concept inspired by field ecology. It refers to evolution towards a "climax community." Not all growth is successional; succession refers to a type of growth that leads to increasing symbiotic diversity. When the term is applied to urban development as a metaphor, it refers to maturing relationships between mutually supportive activities that take place in a delimited locale, such as a neighborhood. It implies convivial social interactions and a diversified local economy, thriving from the mutual support as well as competition. This requires flexibility and agility within the system, enabling small entrepreneurs to easily fill the niches that emerge over time. These niches usually correspond to needed community support and services that help communities to become financially more resilient and self-sufficient.

There are three conditions that establish succession. First is incremental growth; the development or construction process should be able to support the addition of a building or an expansion, one at a time. The compound model enables this. Figure 7.9 provides an example of the succession process of a compound. The construction may begin with one or two buildings, and more can be added in time as the household's finances allow. The second condition is ease in repurposing and remodeling. Note that the changes in the images in Figure 7.9 are due to the addition not just of new buildings, but of annexes and modifications to the current ones. Some terraces are enclosed to become indoor spaces; some porches are added; some detached buildings are attached by a connector. The compounds are to evolve and mature to fulfill new opportunities and to meet the changing needs of the community. The potential of repurposing and remodeling needs to be built into the incremental decision-making and design. Garages, for instance, should be designed to accommodate small businesses, as in the near future we may not own cars as we do today. The ground-floor living areas should be built as a core and shell with panels added for temporary use, if there is any possibility for the space to be used as a future business. The third

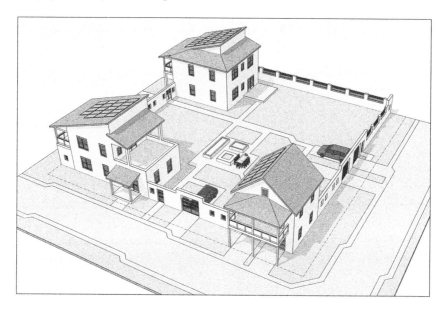

Figure 7.9 Bird's-eye views depicting four possible phases within the succession process of a compound.

Figure 7.9 (Continued)

condition is the presence of a regulatory culture that enables hybrid activities to coexist in support of each other. Coordination of productive activities
and the regulatory processes guiding design and construction need to go
hand in hand at compound and block scales.

Let's illustrate the process with a common scenario at the compound
scale. An older couple buys a compound lot and decides that they don't

need a large house. The y start with a modest dwelling on a corner of the compound. Soon, one of their married adult children decides to join the parents. As a young couple, they are invited to occupy a cottage on the opposite corner. The couple aim to leave their jobs elsewhere and start work in another building within the compound. The removal of a work commute yields extra time for gardening and community involvement, such as representing the family in the block management. In a few years, the family builds additional cottages to rent. Eventually, they expand the office and hire a few employees. The grandfather dies, and the family builds a "granny unit" over their garage so the grandmother can conveniently move into that unit. They rent the grandparents' former house to a young professional who starts practicing from her living room. Eventually, this young professional renovates and rents one of the mews-facing cottages for her small business.

There are many similar possible scenarios. The point is that the compound model, when enabled and supported by a localized management within a dynamic regulatory culture, creates the right conditions for succession of an agile social life along with a diverse set of productive activities at the block scale. It also encourages and enables multigenerational living and aging in place, with residents supporting each other.

Gathering

Meaningful neighborly interaction is a prerequisite for any successful community, and this is especially true of the adaptation village. The physical environment can encourage social interaction by offering centrally located places to gather at each scale, nesting within each other. Gathering places support the kind of social milieu that is essential for the governance system to work and local economy to thrive. The casual socialization encouraged by shared gathering places helps maintain a network of interaction that is essential for managing productive activities. These places encourage person-to-person interaction and are the location of the physically based initiatives at each level of governance. A gathering place also supports the secure place, which is the next design principle, discussed in the following pages.

In the adaptation village, components that nest within each other are configured to accommodate a gathering place as the center or "the heart" of the component (a metaphor Frank Lloyd Wright used as a principle for designing houses). A courtyard is the heart of the compound (Figures 7.4 and 7.5). This is where the residents of the compound socialize, play,

Figure 7.10 A view from a second-story balcony towards the common green and the water tower. Facing the balconies and porches onto the common green enforces its public role and encourages neighborly interaction.

instigate and implement small projects, and discuss issues regarding the life within the compound.

The common green is the heart of the block (Figures 7.2, 7.3, and 7.10) and may contain a community garden as a civic amenity to encourage production and casual interaction. It may also contain a sheltered gathering place such as the one located under the water tower depicted in Figure 7.11. This arrangement may accommodate more formal meetings in addition to casual ones. Such a place may be enclosed and would thus be flexible and suitable for celebrations and even informal commercial activities (such as garage sales and cloths-swapping events). This is where the block management can meet, if not at the main house.

A neighborhood park, where a modestly scaled community house is located, is the heart of the quadrant. Here are larger-scaled amenities that cannot be accommodated at the block scale, such as recreational facilities and gathering halls for various events, most of which are planned and scheduled. Here, in addition to all the above, some educational functions can be accommodated.

The village center, with its centrally located parks and civic buildings, is the heart of the entire adaptation village (Figure 7.12). The facilities within the village center bring all the village residents together and sustain civic life. In addition to daily educational and cultural gatherings, organized seasonal activities need to include celebrations and festivals. Programming and organizing these events require professional commitment and they

Figure 7.11 The gathering place located underneath the water tower. A large dining table together with smaller tables and easy chairs invites gatherings.

Figure 7.12 A bird's-eye view of a weekly farmers' market taking place on one of the streets located in the village center. Drawing by Ronnie Pelusio

need to be part of management's scope. Along with some functions focusing on specialized interests, events aimed at attracting residents with diverse interests need to be organized to strengthen social ties between residents.[2]

Secure Place

Successful settlements feel comfortable and safe. They combine social relationships with gathering places. There is a strong relationship between the strength of social ties and the layout of gathering places in creating and sustaining a secure place, with a sufficient level of security that can be obtained without active policing, but instead relying on "eyes on the street," a term that has been introduced into the vocabulary of urbanism by Jane Jacobs.[3] If there is a sense of ownership of a common space (for instance, if the residents know each other or perhaps are active participants in maintaining it), and if the layout of the space allows residents and business owners to see and observe the space, then the setting tends to be relatively safe. According to Oscar Newman, author of *Defensible Space* (1976), the combination of social and physical factors is crucial for natural deterrence without active policing.[4] These techniques are effective in most American urban environments under most conditions. However, if the level of threat increases, many builders turn to solutions such as gated settlements, fortified compounds, and televised security checkpoints. These solutions are controversial because they preclude open, porous, and pedestrian-friendly traditional neighborhoods. They can also hamper the level of social interaction and sense of community. This brings us to two questions. First is: how much security should an adaptation village plan for? The second question is: which is safer – segregation or integration, isolation or gathering?

Let's start with the first question. Unfortunately, increase in social unrest is a strong possibility in the 21st century. The gap between the haves and have-nots will likely worsen as a consequence of the climate crisis. The level of threat will depend on the location of the adaptation village. The precautionary maxim is to expect the worst and plan for it.

When a disaster hits an area, there appear to be two opposing tendencies among the residents. Some leave their comfort zones to help others, especially when there is a community that supports that response. On the other hand, others retreat and become protective of their territory. This tendency avoids conflict via separation from people unlike themselves. Similarly, distancing and isolation have been the forces behind single-use zoning in suburbia. Yet, such areas are the least self-sufficient and therefore the most vulnerable. Thus, we have the answer to the second question: within the framework of resilience and adaptation, diversity and integration are preferable to isolation and segregation. We need to explore ways to provide protection and security without compromising social contact. Throughout

Figure 7.13 A building with an upper-story loggia from Baeza, Spain. Note how the high garden wall is integrated into the architecture of the building and how it accommodates an opening with a graceful wrought iron grill.

Figure 7.14 A street view from Old Town Datça, Turkey. The tall garden walls are a part of the architecture, creating an appealing and welcoming streetscape.

Figure 7.15 A grilled window from Puerto Val-larta, Mexico. Security measures do not have to communicate hostility. On the contrary, they may be quite appealing.

Figure 7.16 A grilled window from Baeza, Spain. Another example of how a composition primarily aiming at providing security is respectful to the public view.

history, social instability has been a constant with urbanism, but there are sensitive planning techniques from which to draw.

Many of these techniques are incorporated into the adaptation village design. At the scale of the compound, garden walls, fences, and gates are simple, common elements of enclosure that define safe perimeters. These elements have been employed throughout history, especially in the urban vernacular of hot climates where, for instance, garden walls are incorporated into the architecture and an attractive façade composition is achieved (Figures 7.13 and 7.14). In many cases attractive grills are also incorporated into building walls and are a part of the architecture (Figures and 7.15 and 7.16). Even though they are for security, these elements can be quite artistic and double as a "gift" to the public space, encouraging legitimate contact even with strangers (Figures 7.17 and 7.18). They can communicate civic pride and respect.

In the adaptation village, the garden walls separating compounds from each other provide privacy and enclosure for the compound court-yards (Figures 7.19 and 7.20). The garden walls and gates at the perim-

Figure 7.17 A courtyard gate in Cádiz, Spain. Even though providing security is the primary purpose, the composition communicates pride and respects the public.

Figure 7.18 A courtyard gate at Puerto Vallarta, Mexico.

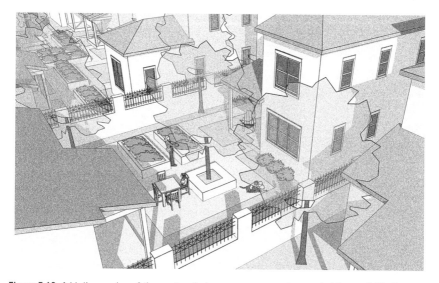

Figure 7.19 A bird's-eye view of the courtyard of a narrow compound separated from neighboring compounds by means of garden walls with grills.

Figure 7.20 An eye-level view of the narrow compound courtyard shown in Figure 7.19.

Figure 7.21 A bird's-eye view of a primary mews façade. Second-story balconies, cottage shop windows, and garden walls with ornamental wrought iron gates provide an attractive, secure, yet friendly frontage along the mews.

eter of each compound work with porches and second-story balconies as part of the architecture and provide an appropriate level of visual transparency to domestic activity. These porches and balconies not only provide "eyes on the mews," but also engage pedestrians and encourage neighborly interaction (Figures 7.21–7.23). The next level of enclosure is provided by the block, which has only four gates that are kept open most of the time to let residents cut through the blocks (Figures 7.24

Figure 7.22 An eye-level view of the same primary mews façade shown in Figure 7.21.

Figure 7.23 A bird's-eye view of a mews façade. Second-story balconies located above the garage entrances are essential to provide eyes on the mews. Note also that there are gates for the off-mews surface parking.

and 7.25). Again, they need to be designed to be appealing and inviting, communicating respect for the block's territory. If need be, the gates can be closed.

The paths that cross through the blocks, the mews, and the streets all provide pedestrian connectivity throughout the village. Higher pedestrian connectivity itself enhances safety. As mentioned earlier, the mews accommodate slight turns and twists instead of being dead straight. These turns along the mews not only make the setting more interesting, they also foster

Figure 7.24 A bird's-eye view of the entrance of a block and the pedestrian path that leads us to the water tower. The entrance is well defined by means of a gate and a graceful garden wall.

Figure 7.25 A closer view of the block gate area shown in Figure 7.24.

surveillance within each segment, especially from the upper-story balconies (Figure 3.21 in Chapter 3). Windows, balconies, and porches, even when there are no residents present, suggest the possibility of eyes on the street to the passerby.

The village center, which is completely open to all, attracts more people, which offers the potential for more eyes on the street. As can be observed in many traditional neighborhoods, attached building types that form a continuous frontage, as does the business row, provide a secure border to the public realm, while maintaining a pedestrian-friendly environment.

The strategies and techniques mentioned thus far in this section are architectural and site planning instruments known to achieve secure places. There are also a wide array of active policing solutions – surveillance, entry control, roving patrols, emergency response, and so on. These are not intrinsic to the physical design of the adaptation village, but may be added if and when the need arises.

Climate-Conscious Design

Both the layout and the buildings of adaptation villages need to respond to the local climatic conditions in order to create comfort zones – places where life is accommodated with a tolerable temperature, air quality, and humidity. The principle of climate-conscious design calls for accomplishing comfort zones without depending on advanced mechanical heating and cooling machinery, which increases our energy consumption and leaves us vulnerable to power outages. Heat waves, when coupled with power shortages, can be fatal wherever the built environment is not shaped to provide comfort zones naturally. This vulnerability is becoming more significant because average temperatures are increasing everywhere, and the regions with hot climates are expanding even further, putting their residents at risk. Building the same buildings in every climate zone, as we currently do, is senseless. We need to learn from the building prototypes evolved to respond to the climate at a time when mechanical systems were not available.

The adaptation village plan presented as a model has been developed for the temperate climate of Colorado's Front Range. The compounds

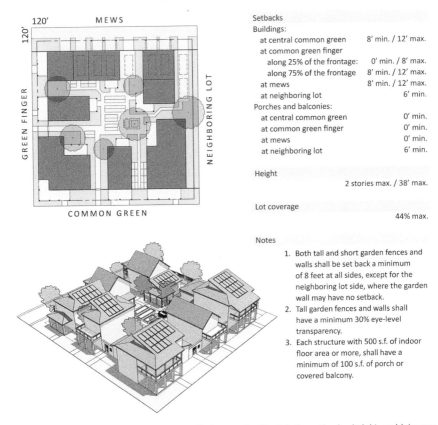

120'   M E W S

120'

GREEN FINGER

NEIGHBORING LOT

COMMON GREEN

Setbacks

Buildings:
at central common green	8' min. / 12' max.
at common green finger	
along 25% of the frontage:	0' min. / 8' max.
along 75% of the frontage	8' min. / 12' max.
at mews	8' min. / 12' max.
at neighboring lot	6' min.

Porches and balconies:
at central common green	0' min.
at common green finger	0' min.
at mews	0' min.
at neighboring lot	6' min.

Height

2 stories max. / 38' max.

Lot coverage

44% max.

Notes

1. Both tall and short garden fences and walls shall be set back a minimum of 8 feet at all sides, except for the neighboring lot side, where the garden wall may have no setback.
2. Tall garden fences and walls shall have a minimum 30% eye-level transparency.
3. Each structure with 500 s.f. of indoor floor area or more, shall have a minimum of 100 s.f. of porch or covered balcony.

Figure 7.26 Front Range compound lot type (for temperate climate): the setbacks, height, and lot coverage restrictions, together with the notes, define this lot type.

illustrated thus far are appropriate for temperate climate zones. The rules that define the essential properties of this prototype form the Front Range compound lot type (Figure 7.26). The detached structures of this compound work well in both temperate and cold climates. However, the compound plan should be revised when employed in hot-arid and hot-humid climates. The lot types titled South West compound (Figure 7.27) and Southern compound (Figure 7.28), provide the essential form-based rules for designing compounds for adaptation villages in hot climates.[5] The regulatory tools that form these lot types are discussed in detail in Appendix A: Tools for Coding (these tools are presented as tables in Figures 7.26–7.28). Here, we briefly summarize their basic characteristics.

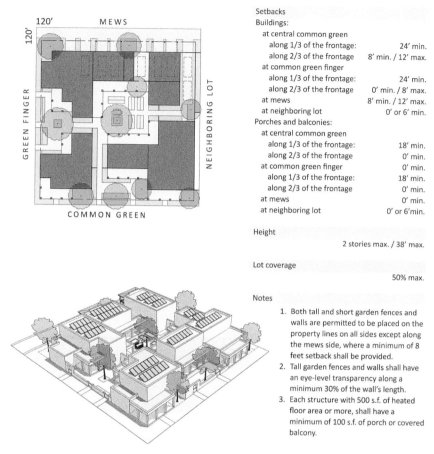

120'   MEWS

120'

GREEN FINGER

NEIGHBORING LOT

COMMON GREEN

Setbacks
Buildings:
  at central common green
    along 1/3 of the frontage: 24' min.
    along 2/3 of the frontage   8' min. / 12' max.
  at common green finger
    along 1/3 of the frontage: 24' min.
    along 2/3 of the frontage   0' min. / 8' max.
  at mews   8' min. / 12' max.
  at neighboring lot   0' or 6' min.
Porches and balconies:
  at central common green
    along 1/3 of the frontage: 18' min.
    along 2/3 of the frontage   0' min.
  at common green finger   0' min.
    along 1/3 of the frontage: 18' min.
    along 2/3 of the frontage   0' min.
  at mews   0' min.
  at neighboring lot   0' or 6'min.

Height
                          2 stories max. / 38' max.

Lot coverage
                                      50% max.

Notes
  1. Both tall and short garden fences and
     walls are permitted to be placed on the
     property lines on all sides except along
     the mews side, where a minimum of 8
     feet setback shall be provided.
  2. Tall garden fences and walls shall have
     an eye-level transparency along a
     minimum 30% of the wall's length.
  3. Each structure with 500 s.f. of heated
     floor area or more, shall have a
     minimum of 100 s.f. of porch or covered
     balcony.

Figure 7.27 South West compound lot type (for hot-arid climate): The setbacks, height, and lot coverage restrictions, together with the notes, define this lot type.

The South West compound is specific to hot-arid and high-desert climates. The design principles include: (a) covering most of the ground area with the building footprints (high lot coverage percentage); (b) attaching buildings to each other to minimize the exterior façades; (c) creating tall, well-shaded courtyards; (d) sealing courtyards during the day to exclude hot breezes; and (e) employing a "wedding cake" kind of a building form with a larger ground floor and a smaller upper floor.[6] Following these principles, the South West compound reduces the size of the main courtyard by moving the buildings closer together, allowing secondary courtyards

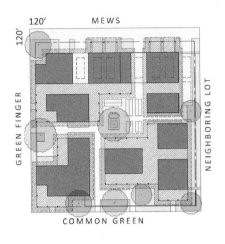

Setbacks
Buildings:
   at central common green
      along 1/3 of the frontage: 24′ min.
      along 2/3 of the frontage   8′ min. / 12′ max.
   at common green finger
      along 1/3 of the frontage: 24′ min.
      along 2/3 of the frontage   0′ min. / 8′ max.
   at mews   8′ min. / 12′ max.
   at neighboring lot   6′ min.
Porches and balconies:
   at central common green
      along 1/3 of the frontage: 18′ min.
      along 2/3 of the frontage   0′ min.
   at common green finger   0′ min.
      along 1/3 of the frontage: 18′ min.
      along 2/3 of the frontage   0′ min.
   at mews   0′ min.
   at neighboring lot   6′ min.

Height
                          2 stories max. / 45′ max.

Coverages
Ground floor footprint   38% max.
Roof   75% min.

Notes
1. Floor area of each footprint shall not exceed 1200 s.f. on the ground floor.
2. Both tall and short garden fences and walls are permitted to be placed on the property lines on all sides except along the mews, where a minimum of 8 feet setback shall be provided.
3. Tall garden fences and walls shall have an eye-level transparency along a minimum 70% of the wall's length.
4. Each structure with 500 s.f. of heated floor area or more, shall have a minimum of 100 s.f. of porch or covered balcony.

Figure 7.28 Southern compound lot type (for hot-humid climate): The setbacks, height, and lot coverage restrictions, together with the notes, define this lot type.

at the periphery. Buildings are connected also by means of galleries with moveable screens that can prevent air movement during the day and allow it in the evening. Flat roofs are employed as they reflect the heat back to the sky.

The Southern compound shown in Figure 7.28 is for hot-humid climates. A few of the primary design principles are: (a) providing multiple breezeways by detaching buildings and employing outdoor verandas;

(b) employing an upside-down "wedding cake" kind of a building form with limited ground floor footprint; (c) connecting buildings under large roofs with large eaves to maximize shade; and (d) employing large eaves.

Following these principles, the Southern compound lot type reduces the size of the courtyard further, but increases the amount of shaded areas (hatched areas on the lot diagram in Figure 7.28). On the ground floor, there are multiple footprints detached from each other to create the essential breezeways – these are well-lived covered verandas and patios.[7] Note that nine footprints on the ground floor are gathered under only four roofs (Figure 7.28). The area of the lot directly open to the sky is limited.

These two lot types exemplify climate-conscious design for hot-arid and hot-humid climates. However, there are climatic variations for each specific location. Compound plans need to be adjusted for each. One of the most important adjustments is the size of the courtyard, which gets smaller and deeper as the climatic conditions grow more severe (much like a camera's diaphragm that controls the shutter aperture; the higher the amount of light, the smaller the aperture). The sections that cut through courtyards with various widths, presented in Figures 7.29 and 7.30, show how courtyard size can be calibrated in hot-arid and hot humid climate zones, depending on the severity of the conditions.

The site plan provided for the village center is also a response to the temperate climate of Colorado's Front Range: warm, dry summers and cold winters with snowfall but with many sunny days. The village center is oriented north–south, which minimizes north-facing sidewalks where the sun cannot reach to melt ice in winter (Figure 3.2). The east-facing sidewalks along the business row receive sun in the morning, and the west-facing sidewalks receive it in the afternoon. The plan is tilted 10° to increase eastern exposure and reduce western exposure, because it takes longer for the morning sun to heat surfaces, whereas the afternoon sun is more intense and heats surfaces faster. This orientation matters the most at the center because of the business row, which is a wall of buildings that creates continuous shadow on the sidewalk. In the neighborhoods, there are gaps between buildings to bring sunlight into the compounds. The orientation and configuration of the village center need to be revised when it is employed in hot climates.

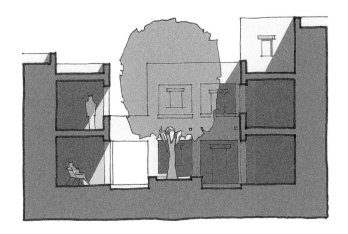

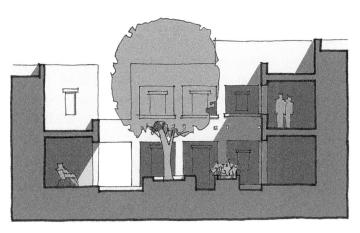

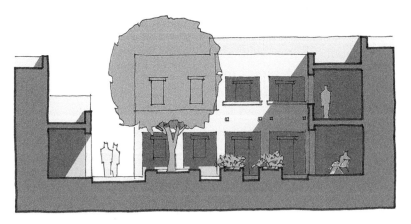

Figure 7.29 Cross sections through three compounds located within a hot-arid climate zone. As the conditions become more severe, the size of the courtyard gets narrower (from bottom to top).

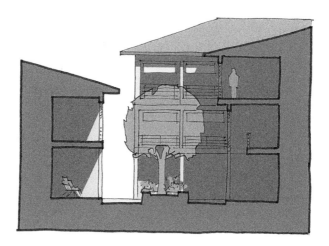

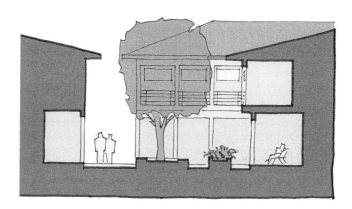

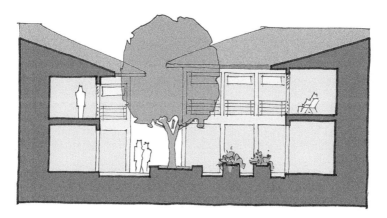

Figure 7.30 Cross sections through three compounds located within a hot-humid climate zone. As the conditions become more severe, the size of the courtyard gets narrower (from bottom to top).

Notes

1   The rural-to-urban transect has been tested in a score of urban planning projects by the planning firms Duany Plater-Zyberk & Company, Hellmuth, Obata + Kassabaum (HOK Group, Inc.), Torti Gallas, Dover, Kohl, Placemakers, Pel-Ona Architects and Urbanists, and many others, on both greenfield and infill sites. For an in-depth exploration of the theory and application of the concept of transect in urbanism, see Duany and Falk (2020). See also Duany and Brain (Eds.) (2005). The urban-to-rural transect introduced by Duany Plater-Zyberk & Company has six transects: (T1) natural (or rural preserve), (T2) rural reserve, (T3) suburban, (T4) general urban, (T5) urban center, and (T6) urban core. The adaptation village does not include "urban center" and "urban core" transects. For further resources on the subject, visit the Center for Applied Transect Studies at https://transect.org/

2   For instance, instead of organizing a festival of music only, gathering together a cluster of events – music, other arts, food, craft, etc. – under a unifying theme (such as spring festival, colors festival, diversity festival, etc.) works better by attracting residents with diverse interests and strengthening the social ties between residents at the scale of the adaptation village.

3   We are indebted to Jane Jacobs for the introduction of the ubiquitous term "eyes on the street" to the language of urbanism (see Jacobs, 1961).

4   Any reader who is interested in the subject should read, if she or he hasn't done so yet, Chapter 2, "The Uses of Sidewalk: Safety," in Jane Jacobs's *The Death and Life of Great American Cities* (1961). Even though his theories have created many controversies, Oscar Newman's *Defensible Space* (1972) is still another landmark book. See also Cisneros (1995) for a practical interpretation of the defensible space theory.

5   For further discussion on the lot types approach to drafting form-based codes, see Onaran (2019).

6   Here is further explanation for these design principles. In hot-arid regions, there are significant temperature changes not only between the day and night, but also between surfaces exposed to the sun and those that are not. In the vernacular of hot-arid climate zones, buildings are usually attached to each other and face only small courtyards and narrow streets. The courtyards and narrow streets are the only outdoor spaces left untouched by building footprints, eliminating exterior façades exposed to the sun. In hot-arid climates, paved areas, when not shaded, can easily create heat islands. Providing narrow, tall courtyards (where the width is smaller than the height) is the most effective way to create a shaded area with its own micro-climate. The "wedding cake" form, with large ground floors and smaller upper floors, is designed to catch the evening breezes. In terms of the breezes in hot-arid regions, air movement should be blocked during the day so that the shaded micro-climates (such as those created in courtyards) are protected from hot winds and breezes. In the evening, however, when the air cools down, air movement should be maximized to allow the cool air to flow into the courtyards and interior spaces. This is the same principle with the whole-house fans most of us are familiar with: you open all the windows and shutters after dark and run the house fan to pull the cool outside air through the building. Then, in the morning, you close all the windows and shutters to allow the cool air to stay in the building all day. For further explanation, please see the term "comfort zone" in Appendix B: Essential Terms and Concepts for Adaptation Urbanism.

7   Here is further explanation for these design principles. In hot-humid climates, humidity holds the heat close to the ground and doesn't allow surfaces to emit the heat back to the sky easily. When there is humidity in the air, the sun reaches and heats up the ground at a slower rate, but, once heated, the surfaces cannot cool down easily because the humidity holds the heat. The only way to cool heated areas then is to move the air, that is, to create breezes. As in the hot-arid regions, creating shade in hot-humid regions is essential for

comfort but is not enough in itself; air movement needs to be created. As a matter of fact, as it is so hard to cool down surfaces once heated, creating shade is much more important for hot-humid climates. In other words, preventing surfaces from heating up in the first place is essential. Careful landscaping and shaded water features are two means used for cooling down the air. However, it is the air movement that maximizes any such cooling effect. Detaching buildings from each other, with limited distances between, helps move the air. Smaller gaps in between buildings are much more desirable because such spaces can work as breeze funnels and create breezeways. Buildings close to each other, with large overhangs, create shade and air movement. Mazelike hollow buildings, touching the ground in limited ways and organized under large roofs, are ideal. Layouts that trap air movement are most problematic. For further explanation, please see the term "comfort zone" in Appendix B: Essential Terms and Concepts for Adaptation Urbanism.

8

LIFE IN THE 21ST CENTURY

We are living in an era of rapid change. The world we live in today is different than the one we lived a month or two ago. Even though it has been only 2 years, it feels as if our lives before the pandemic were of a different era. Some of these changes are ominous, such as the forest wildfires, floods, droughts, storms – all in never-seen-before intensities. There are also some structural changes happening fast: the increasing acidity of the oceans, erosion of fertile topsoil, melting ice caps, contamination of fresh water sources, thawing permafrost, and so on. Now (at the time of writing this book), we are living with a pandemic, and its imposed lifestyle changes and societal transformations will most probably stay with us, even when the majority of the planet's population are vaccinated. What are these changes? How do they fit with the adaptation principles reviewed thus far? Answering these questions is the focus of this chapter. There are three major strategies that resulted in societal transformations which are significant for adaptation. These are working from home, podding, and contact tracing.

Working from Home

The average breadwinner nowadays works 40–50 hours a week or more, away from home, usually with a significant amount of time spent commuting. The remaining time is reserved for socialization, family, and then, if any time is left, hobbies. It is very common to think of hobbies as endeavors to enjoy and take pleasure in, and work as an obligation. Those of us in the

 DOI: 10.4324/9781003182627-8

West who live with the Protestant work ethic and spirit of capitalism have become obsessed with not wasting our time with anything but worthwhile production. In order to be able to monitor our work, we have separated places of work from the places where we live. We have rationalized and systematized our activities of production and developed tools to monitor how we use our time at work.[1]

However, this picture is out of balance and is not resilient. We realize this when we lose our jobs: suddenly, life becomes very difficult. The importance of diversifying one's productive endeavors to achieve financial resilience is an important lesson some of us learned during the financial crisis of 2008–2009. Many who had lost jobs ventured into smaller and more agile business endeavors and learned how to practice with modest means. More than 10 years later, we are remembering the same lesson, but this time with a slight variation: jobs are being lost not because of an economic downturn but because of the restrictions that the pandemic imposed on certain businesses. Jobs have been lost in the business sectors that depended on social contact, such as service, entertainment, performing arts, tourism, travel, and so on. The workforce in most other industries has learned how to minimize in-person contacts and work from home. We soon realized the strengths and weaknesses of our living arrangements and adopted accordingly. We have managed to put together computer nooks, office corners, and workshop spaces in our homes in various creative ways. In spite of the difficulties, such as needing silence for internet meetings and living with kids full-time, we started to see the advantages as well: not commuting, having more flexibility in our work schedule, and finding time for other productive endeavors.

Even though the introduction of work- and business-related activities into our homes happened by necessity, it proved to be not only possible but also desirable, and most probably will continue in the future. This observation is strong enough to change the zoning paradigm that focuses on creating single-use neighborhoods and sprawl. Many municipalities are already relaxing their exclusionary regulations to encourage, or at least not ban, more hybrid uses within our neighborhoods. It is not unrealistic to hope that the kind of regulatory culture advocated in this book for the adaptation village will become the norm of the future. This is a good time to argue for (a) subsidiarity in land use controls and building code enforcement and (b) agility and flexibility in construction processes. It is usually difficult to change certain assumptions and their corresponding rules once they have been taken for granted for decades within the bureaucracies of the city halls. But the experience of living with this pandemic has already brought into question the primary assumption of exclusionary zoning that claims most other uses disturb residential use and therefore should be excluded from residential neighborhoods. Even the most conservatist zoning bureaucrat is ready to reconsider this assumption today. This is the right time for a reform.

One other important implication of the working-from-home experience is the relaxation of the territorial controls that employers use to monitor the production process. When there is an office space, the time spent in it is labor; it is monitored and paid for accordingly. In the absence of the office or the work space, an employer needs to trust the employee and monitor the outcome or the product instead, not the time spent in the office, even if the fees are still paid per hour. This difference has been significant, especially for larger production systems that depend on high levels of efficiencies. Many businesses needed to loosen their schedules to adapt to the reality of the new social distancing restrictions.[2] As a consequence, we have experienced some "slack" in certain markets that would otherwise be "taut," terms used by David Fleming, who sees slack as a condition of the localized markets of the coming generations and a necessary principle for surviving the future. He names the localized markets of the future "lean economies" and suggests that (a) trust in the local economy, (b) product diversity, and (c) multiple aims beyond profit maximization shall form and enable the lean economies.[3] These changes, though at modest levels, are already occurring because of the condition of working from home. The key point is to see slack in the markets not as a weakness, but as a value that enables adaptation. Similarly, trust in local economies, product diversity, and multiple aims beyond profit are the objectives for lean economies within the framework of adaptation. The last of these three, multiple aims, needs a further emphasis: This is a point that takes us away from simple profit-oriented rationalism and not only emphasizes other civic obligations, including the environment and local justice, equity, and so forth, but also underlines working together and strengthening communal ties as prerequisites for lean economies.

Podding

The social distancing and isolation imposed by the pandemic impacted the well-being of the public in a negative way. Unlike other disasters where people usually react by investing in communal ties more readily than during usual times, the pandemic drastically transformed social relations and made life lonely and difficult. According to a study published by NORC at the University of Chicago, the number of Americans experiencing serious psychological distress tripled between March and July 2020.[4] The study also stated that the frequency of feeling lonely correlated with exposure to the coronavirus, either personally or geographically, in highly impacted areas. This indicates that the stronger the restrictions imposing isolation, the more likely people will loosen their caution and be less diligent when given the opportunity. This implies a vicious cycle in terms of public health policy.

Podding – forming social groups of trust where members limit their person-to-person contacts outside the group, with the aim of keeping the group safe – has been a good strategy, as opposed to social isolation, during the pandemic. Also known as "quaranteams" and bubbles, pods are small groups formed not only for socialization but also for support. In terms of the pattern of social relations, unlike the multiple open-contact networks that household members freely sustained, podding works with a small, closed group. Since the social needs of a household can be diverse (kids needing to socialize with other kids, elders needing care and companionship, working parents needing child care, adolescents needing inspiration, and most adults needing sexual desire as part of being alive and healthy), the more diverse the members of a pod, the better it functions as a support group.[5] Groups who share certain amenities and live together, such as cohousing communities, have created pods easily. Others who live in single-use neighborhoods and are already isolated and distanced physically struggle to form successful pods. They also struggle to receive some of the daily support services (child care, house cleaning, simple repairs, house-call health services, etc.), because many of these services require in-person contact with a stranger.

The compound model enables the formation of social pods. In addition to providing financial resilience for the household, the compound brings together a small group of residents with diverse demographics and interests who can support each other in various ways. When the productive activities within the compound are coordinated with other compounds on the block and managed by the block-level administration, this mutual assistance reaches a larger network, with more constructive support in terms of sustaining a strong local economy. In other words, creating concentric circles of trust at compound and block scales opens up many possibilities for increased mutual support and self-sufficiency. This is resilience not only in the face of system failures, but also, as we have now learned, in the face of future pandemics. Concentric circles of trust nesting within each other, as opposed to increased isolation, loneliness, and psychological distress, will sustain public health better, despite future pandemics. This is how a symbiotic relationship can be established between lean economies and public health policies.

Contact Tracing

Contact tracing has been another effective public health policy in addressing the pandemic. It refers to identifying persons who may have come into contact with an infected person and the subsequent collection of further information about these contacts. By tracing the contacts of infected individuals, testing them for infection, quarantining the infected, and tracing their contacts in turn, public health agencies aim to reduce infections in the population. Even though it has been effective in communities with relatively close contact networks, the effectiveness of contract tracing diminishes when dealing with groups with more open, large-scale social contact networks – when, for instance, we trace groups who travel globally. This is the reason why we have been experiencing many travel restrictions during the pandemic.

One important lesson we have learned from our contact tracing experiences is that localization of social contacts provides resiliency. Considering that we may experience other pandemics in the near future, localizing social contacts may be, not just by choice but also by necessity, the predominant lifestyle of the 21st century. There are three categories of contacts in our modern societies: (a) we socialize and exchange digital content via the internet; (b) we communicate, buy, and sell via mail (where we physically touch a letter or a product that arrives through the mail); and (c) we socialize and engage in commerce via in-person contact. Even though contact tracing focuses on the last category only, it is eye-opening to review how this pandemic has affected all three of these categories. As compared with pre-pandemic times, internet socialization has increased significantly. Not only casual social contacts, but also business meetings, educational interactions, and even certain governmental assemblies (such as city council and planning commission meetings) are now conducted via the internet. It is reasonable to expect that this trend will continue, especially in sustaining distant global contacts. However, it may not be prudent to take our internet for granted. Depending on it for the essential functioning of a business is risky if we consider the possibility of a future system collapse, or even a temporary power outage, which is not a distant possibility, as noted earlier. Nevertheless, a certain level of internet support can be established locally via mesh networks to continue functioning through power outages.

As for the second category, the volume of commerce via mail has also increased during the pandemic. Many of us, isolating ourselves at home, depend on mail delivery. This, however, created difficult conditions for the postal service employees, as well as supply center workers for large mail-order businesses: the infection rates went up among them. Since increased infection rates in one group affect the whole society, depending on mail delivery is not the most sustainable public health strategy for our future. Furthermore, mail delivery, especially of goods traveling long distances, may be interrupted during future climate disasters.

As for the last category, in-person contacts, even though avoiding them is the ultimate solution for prevention of infections, as noted above, it is not a realistic one. Limiting in-person contacts to closed groups, however, is an effective solution. Podding works. Contact tracing also works if our social, as well as business, relations are localized. This brings us to the governance and social order principles of adaptation. In the face of inevitable future industrial downscaling and economic degrowth, localization of the governance, social order, and economy is not only a sustainable solution but also the one that enables us to thrive. It is a solution and a necessary condition for life in the rest of our difficult upcoming century.

Notes

1 Here, in order not to lose our focus, we have presented a very simplified and shortened version of the relationship between a Calvinist work ethic and the rationalization and systematization of the production process. The subject is discussed further at the end of the book in Appendix B: Terms and Concepts for Adaptation Urbanism, under the term "enjoyment." For a deeper and more comprehensive discussion, we suggest Max Weber's (1991; the original work was published in 1905) landmark work *The Protestant Ethic and Spirit of Capitalism*. Also, especially for the effect of this rationalization and systematization on our territorial control strategies, please refer to David R. Sack's (1986) book *Human Territoriality: Its theory and history*.

2 In the absence of high levels of efficiency, it is reasonable to expect that some large businesses, especially the ones that function at a global scale, may need to downsize. We are already observing some of this. See, for instance, Thomas, Chaney, and Cutter (2020).

3 The three points mentioned are a part of a seven-point protocol for lean economies. The other four are: (1) a small number of buyers and sellers, (2) barriers to entry and exit, (3) barriers to mobility, and (4) imperfect knowledge; all have been observed temporarily

within isolated economies in disaster areas. For further discussion, see *Surviving the Future* by David Fleming (2016b).

4 The study mentioned is the COVID Response Tracking Study prepared by NORC at the University of Chicago (Sterrett and Smith, 2020). It is retrievable from: www.norc. org/Research/Projects/Pages/covid-response-tracking-study.aspx

5 For more information about forming pods see Smith and Winters (2020).

9
CONCLUSION

The future is dark and uncertain. The recent pandemic is a glimpse of the difficulties we will need to live with in the near future. The climate crisis challenges us at an unprecedented, urgent scale. We will most probably experience disruptions in supply lines and large-scale sustenance systems that have supported our lives. Some of us will relocate to avoid the difficulties. Where will we relocate to? And how will we live when we get there? Disasters such as Hurricane Katrina showed that, when not prepared, authorities react mostly in panic, in ways that are not always efficient and are often unfair and resistant to enabling local resources and local communal capabilities, which is the opposite of establishing the systems of resilience that would prepare us for future catastrophes. We, the planners and urbanists – the trained experts – have the responsibility to show that there are other options. We must expect the worst and plan for it. Thus, it has been this book's objective to convince us all that a system of resilience can be achieved by investing in ways of living that foster human life and enable people to be productive and mutually supportive. This can be achieved via lean local economies that can sustain life at a scale as small as a walking shed, rather than depending on large-scale sustenance systems that are likely to fail. We have proposed practical policies and strategies aiming at achieving this.

Making moving away from danger a financially and socially attractive option is the responsibility of – and must be a priority for – all planners and policy makers. Leaving the doomed behind or driving people out after

DOI: 10.4324/9781003182627-9

a disaster is irresponsible. Democratic planning does not force, but rather provides attractive options. Moving away from danger can be practically enabled by adopting new-generation comprehensive plans that create receiving zones. These receiving zones will be instrumental in creating more resilient lives via the following four policy applications:

(a) creating and encouraging more productive ownership models within the receiving zones via solutions such as compounds (integrating this model into zoning ordinances)

(b) establishing preferential tax treatment, such as opportunity zones, to diversify new, local businesses within the receiving zones

(c) adopting tax deduction programs for renting within receiving zones for those breadwinners who live close to their work and rent from an owner who lives on the same lot

(d) providing governmental subsidies for localized infrastructure.

The climate crisis offers an opportunity for people to live better, while being more prepared for the circumstances ahead. Avoiding danger does not just involve, say, avoiding fire or flood, but, by resilience, achieving self-sufficiency. This requires localization of sustenance systems and agility in local governance that can form strong local economies. Thus, a resilient community needs strong social ties between the residents in an environment where they share, give, and enjoy their social lives. The sustenance systems (energy, water, food, waste, and essential goods) need to be localized, but so does governance and the entrepreneurial system. The principle of subsidiarity provides the autonomy to manage these sustenance systems. This kind of community needs a physical environment that is constantly evolving and adjusting to increase symbiotic relations between various productive activities. Specific solutions will likely vary from place to place, but the basic principles (nesting, transect, succession, gathering, secure place, and climate-conscious design) define the DNA of such an adaptive environment focused on localization of sustenance systems. Thus, the three legs of the adaptation action framework, in a nutshell, are:

- localization of sustenance systems
- a governance and social order that can manage the localized systems, and

- design principles that can guide the creation of a physical environment that matches and enables both localization of sustenance systems and the kind of governance and social order that can manage them.

Owing to our urban development history in the United States, the subject of localization usually brings forward questions of exclusivity, elitism, and segregation; getting away from the hustle and bustle and living somewhere isolated, in homogeneous single-use districts has been a primary strategy to avoid conflict. This has created the segmented urban landscapes of sprawl. Exclusivity has been perceived as a prerequisite for security. Providing more governing autonomy for these isolated communities meant that they could distance and isolate themselves further, which contributed to regionally un-equal distribution of certain social services and resources. This is how and why the subsidiarity principle has been associated with segregation by many historians. Because of this cultural and historical background, we expect negative reactions to this book's recommendations; we expect some readers will assume that the localization aimed at creating self-sufficiencies implies exclusivity and segregation. There are two mistakes in this assumption:

(a) Self-sufficiency and localization aren't necessarily aimed at isola-tion, but at surviving through isolation if and when it is imposed by disruptions in large-scale sustenance networks. The principle of nesting, in fact, systematically supports interactions with regional and global systems, but does not depend, at all times, on them alone. There is no reason why a self-sufficient entity cannot support another one. The objective is to create a system where self-sufficient entities interact with each other and create a network of lean economies.

(b) Caring for others because others are needed to play their parts is inherent in self-sufficiency. Self-sufficiency implies diversity and inclusivity as opposed to homogeneity and exclusivity. In the Old Testament, Noah brought a female and male from each species into his ark so that biodiversity could be sustained for life after the flood. This myth must be one of the earliest testaments to what we have been discussing throughout this book: diversity is essential to survive the storm. We need each other. People need access to most kinds of talent, craft, and knowledge in the vicinity. The more diverse the neighborhood we live in, the less vulnerable we will be. The likelihood is high that, in the near future, we will depend on each other to survive as we did in earlier, simpler, but equally fraught, times. Getting along with our neighbors will not be a matter of personal preference anymore, but a matter of necessity.

This brings us to three important conclusions. The first is that, when and if large-scale systems fail, we will need a diverse set of services within close proximity. Second, this can be sustained only through strong local economies that are highly intentional and diverse. And third, inclusivity is essential to this level of diversity.

Even though the future brings many challenges, there are ways to thrive while addressing them. We have an opportunity to create resilient communities through practical steps. Moving away from the danger, if presented as a rational process, opens the door for the opportunity for a landscape of self-sufficiencies, with a network of lean economies supporting each other and enabling us to be creative, productive, and motivated to engage, enjoy, and support each other. This is not a distant utopia, but a very practical and immediate opportunity. We need to grab it. It is our responsibility to grab it.

AFTERWORD

Flood, fire, drought, windstorm, heat wave, and disruption. These are not the *causes* of climate change, they are the *consequences* of climate change. The causes of climate change must be dealt with in *worldwide* agreements; the consequences can be dealt with in *local* agreements. The tools presented in this book can deal directly with adapting to *all* the consequences, but only, and usually indirectly, with mitigating *some* of the causes.

The tools of adaptation are: communities in receiving areas, intentionally organized for diversity in local (15-minute city) balanced, nested community scales, subsidiary governance, and rural-to-urban transect-based calibration of all the above variables.

And what of the argument that high-tech advances can save us from the consequences of climate change? There is no gainsaying that technology (such as life sciences discoveries or the social decentralization of blockchain) continues to advance at a rapid pace, but it is challenging to predict what these technological advances may garner. However, modern technology depends heavily upon the status quo of fragile global systems that are extremely vulnerable to climate change-induced disruptive events. Disruptions interfere with the systems of the status quo and will have devastating effects on technological progress. Adaptation should embrace whatever works to forward the survival of humans and the planetary ecological systems that they share with other fauna and flora.

One could say that effective adaptation will balance localized permaculture systems with new advances. Local permaculture balanced with modern advances will generate adaptation communities that will be:

- *stimulated by* climate change-induced problems, the solution to which is a viable legacy
- *subject to* values of energy conservation, self-reliance, harmonious human occupancy, and economy
- *mediated by* consideration of long-term biosocial factors that can be implemented incrementally
- *achieved by* research and consultation with local governments, clients, and investors, assisting people to gain an education in design and adaptation
- *refined by* allowing space, finance, and feedback to adjust activity, allowing for new or overlooked needs and resources as they occur and pulling residents into the concept as participators
- *leading to* a dynamic and healthy community inhabited by people with the power and understanding to make necessary changes
- *resulting in* the stability of dynamic local adjustment.

This book has been in the making for many years and has had the assistance of many hands. For me, it began with assisting Andrés Duany in writing a White Paper in November 2011 titled "The Questionable Ethics of Ecological Footprinting." Since then, the numerous listserve discussions, side research projects, workshops, presentations, and debates are beyond counting. Andrés Duany has been the leading inspiration for this book and has long been an inspiration and mentor to me and many others. I liken him to a speeding comet that sheds innovative ideas in a long tail and encourages others to take them on and add flesh to their armature. We can thank Korkut Onaran for having the talent and persistence to take this essential idea to the finish line.

Paul Crabtree, PE, CNU-A

Appendix A
Tools for Coding

This appendix provides a selection of basic tools that can be useful for creating a development code that can guide the construction of, and manage the land uses in, the adaptation village. Even though the details of the code and of the review processes will depend on the regulatory context where development will be implemented, we believe that a transect-based code using a diversity of lot types should constitute the main framework for creating a healthy and productive regulation culture.[1]

It is important to craft and structure the code review and code enforcement processes to be dynamic, agile, and consistent with the subsidiarity principle of governance. Thus, this appendix begins with a discussion of code enforcement, management, and monitoring. Next are density and use regulation recommendations for the transects introduced in Chapter 7. Finally, we provide tools to regulate the building form. These tools include lot types and related rules of measurement and, importantly, definitions of the terms used.

Code Enforcement, Management, and Monitoring

The development code for the adaptation village needs to be dynamic; it needs to be seen not as a preconceived static document to be enforced by a top–down authority, such as a municipality, but as an evolving language spoken by the block-, business row-, and village-scale managements to (a) guide the construction, (b) manage day-to-day enforcement of the land use restrictions, and (c) monitor the productive activities within the block and business row to maximize synergies between them. The code enforcement needs to merge into the management of daily activities at local scales. Even though the details of the procedural structures will differ depending on the location and the context, subsidiarity should be the guiding principle for structuring the review processes. For instance, building and occupancy permits for certain simple structures (determined by size, complexity and other criteria) may be issued by the block and business row managements. Permits for larger and more complex structures may be issued by the village and district managements. There may be multiple tiers in review processes as well; the block management may review and recommend approval of certain projects to the village or district management, and village and district managements may issue the final approval. There are many possibilities. If the adaptation village happens to be a part of a municipality, only very limited permitting should be performed by the municipality.

The subsidiarity principle should be applied for conflict resolution as well: only the conflicts that are not resolved at block or business row scales should go to the village management, and only those that are not resolved at village or district management scale should go to a municipality, if there is one. This system may seem radically different than what we are accustomed to, but examples of similar procedural structures do exist. As mentioned before, planned communities are often managed by a hierarchy of multiple homeowners associations (HOAs), where different rules are enforced at different scales. Similarly, in many cities, it is common to see certain building form-related restrictions merged with management of business-specific activities and they are enforced by the business organizations. What may be unusual about the adaptation village is the diversity of productive activities and the management of the localized utilities.

The point is that code enforcement needs to be a part of the management conducted by those who are most familiar with the needs and day-to-day activities of the locality. Under this arrangement – unlike many outdated rules that we currently have in our zoning ordinances that, for instance, prevent perfectly reasonable coexistence of various activities – building and use restrictions would not prevent autonomous creativity; rather, they would contribute to the vitality and strength of the community life. Merging code enforcement with management of community activities implies a dynamic decision-making and problem-solving process where the code is revised when needed. This resembles a system that is closer to common law. The code needs to be seen as an evolving language, not as a rigid final design to be implemented. The specific coding recommendations provided here should be seen within the framework of a dynamic regulation culture.

Densities and Uses

Calibrating the development density in the adaptation village is important, especially when localization of sustenance systems is the primary goal. There may be different levels of localization and self-sufficiencies for different densities and contexts. Our purpose is twofold: (a) to find the sweet spot and (b) to demonstrate how this density can be distributed over the transects. As discussed in Chapter 3, the adaptation village model has three primary components: neighborhoods, village center, and support districts. We present our coding recommendations following the order of these components.

Neighborhoods

Compounds are the basic elements in an adaptation village. They form the blocks, and blocks form the quadrants and neighborhoods, and so forth. Creating a gradation of density for compounds across the transects should be the guiding principle for the way the code addresses densities. We suggest two measures for controlling densities: the number of footprints (or buildings) and the total building floor area permitted on each lot. Below is a simple rule of measurement for "total building floor area." Here is a suggested definition:

- **Total building floor area**: the building floor area on a lot shall be measured to the outside of the framing, not including the exterior cladding material, and shall include all indoor floor areas with a height of 6 feet or greater, regardless of use. Neither garages nor basements shall be counted towards total building floor area.

Table A.1 Number of Footprints Permitted in Compounds per Lot Size and Transect

Minimum lot size	Inner Ring Neigh. Transect	Middle Ring Neigh. Transect	Peripheral Neigh. Transect
120' x 120'	6	5	4
80' x 120'	4	3	2
60' x 120'	3	2	-
40' x 120'	2	-	-

Table A.2 Maximum Total Floor Areas Permitted at Compounds per Lot Size and Transect

Minimum lot size	Inner Ring Neigh. Transect	Middle Ring Neigh. Transect	Peripheral Neigh. Transect
120' x 120'	9000 sf	8500 sf	8000 sf
80' x 120'	7000 sf	5500 sf	4500 sf
60' x 120'	4500 sf	4000 sf	-
40' x 120'	3000 sf	-	-

Note: Total floor area does not include garages and basements

Tables A.1 and A.2 provide suggested maximum numbers of footprints and the total building floor areas per lot, respectively. These tables are organized according to the lot sizes and the transects that were introduced in Chapter 7. Figure 7.8 (Chapter 7) illustrates what these table summarize; it provides nine lot diagrams organized according to the permitted lot sizes within each transect. Note that the smaller lot sizes are not permitted within middle ring and peripheral neighborhood transects, which is consistent with the density gradation. Tables A.1 and A.2 make more sense when we study the lot diagrams presented in Figure 7.8. Even though the numbers of footprints demonstrated in Figure 7.8 represent the maximums, the building sizes are not the maximums, but they show a probable and more realistic outcome. It is important to emphasize that, even in smaller compounds with fewer footprints, the courtyards still work well as gathering places.

Regarding the uses, any code that aims to increase conviviality and the diversity of productive activities (so that synergies between them are maximized) needs to suggest ways to accommodate uses together, harmoniously, instead of excluding them. This is particularly crucial for the compounds. Even though residential may be the predominant use, compounds cannot be treated as single-use zone districts; they need to accommodate a diversity of uses in such a way that they can coexist without disturbing each other. This can be achieved by introducing a few simple performance standards to the definitions of the use categories that will be assigned for the compounds. The following use category definitions aim at making it easier for these uses to be accommodated with others through reducing their impacts by controlling their size, character, performance, and management.

- **Cottage industry and retail**: premises available for the creation, assembly, and repair of artifacts (including carpentry, ironwork, and similar crafts), as well as cooking and food preparation, including their retail sale as long as produced, performed, or managed by the residents of the compound (or the block). The premises reserved for these functions shall not exceed 1,600 square feet per lot. Cottage industry and retail shall be conducted so as not to attract more than ten customers or clients to the compound at any time.
- **Cottage farming**: premises available for small-scale farming to support the residents of a lot, with limited surplus. Only pre-approved organic pesticides and herbicides are permitted. Raising and maintaining cows, pigs, goats, sheep, and hens are permitted by review and approval by the block management. Use of machinery creating noise levels more than 40 dB shall be limited to daylight hours. Use of machinery heavier than 4 tons or creating noise levels more than 65 dB is not permitted. Larger machines that belong to the village or district management are permitted to be employed on a limited basis.
- **Home occupation**: premises available for conducting business in a dwelling, or in a building on the lot where the dwelling is located, by one or more permanent residents of the lot. The home occupation shall be conducted so as not to attract more than ten customers or clients to the lot at any time.

The performance standards included in these definitions are provided as a reference point and need be adjusted by each block management according to the customs and needs of the residents. For instance, some block managements may agree to a few larger businesses if the block residents see these businesses as beneficial. A finer gradation of use controls may also be preferred by block managements, where only *home occupation* is permitted on common court and common green finger frontages, and *cottage industry* and *retail* are permitted only in mews frontages. Depending on the context of the adaptation village, the village management may choose to set these standards according to the transects: larger and more intense *home occupation*, *cottage industry*, and *retail* uses on inner and middle ring neighborhood transects, and larger and more intense *cottage farming* activities on the peripheral transect. Another way to increase the capacity of cottage farming on the peripheral neighborhood transect is to encourage inclusion of some ancillary activities in the common greens of the blocks. These may be special events including, but not limited to, food craft festivals, farmers markets, petting zoos, and cooking and permaculture classes. Some of these activities have land use implications, and the code needs to clarify that they are permitted on certain blocks.

Village Center

The village center includes the central parks, civic buildings, and business row. Chapter 7 discusses the size, use, and character of the civic buildings – they will vary depending on the context of the adaptation village. Here, for the purposes of the development code, we will focus on the business row only.

The business row brings together several building types that accommodate a variety of uses (for a reminder, see Figure 3.11). Table A.3 provides a set of regulations for these building types. The first line on the table reads "building size," which lists the maximum total building floor areas permit-

Table A.3 Lot Types for Business Row Building Types

	FLEX SPACE	HIDDEN COURT	LIVE-ABOVE	MAIN STREET BUILDING
Building size:	5000 s.f. max.	3000 s.f. max.	2500 s.f. max.	5000 s.f. max.
Setbacks:				
At street	12' min. / 15' max.	see note 1	see note 2	see note 3
At mews	8' min.	8' min.	8' min.	see note 4
At green	6' min.	6' min.	6' min.	6' min.
As side	0' or 6' min.	see note 5	0' or 6' min.	0' or 6' min.
Height:	2 stories / 32' max.	2 stories / 38' max.	3 stories / 45' max.	3 stories / 45' max.

Notes:

1. Street setback for the Hidden Court shall be 4 feet minimum / 8 feet maximum for the ground floor, 24 feet minimum for the second and third stories.
2. Street setback for the Live-Above shall be 4 feet minimum / 8 feet maximum for the ground floor, 12 feet minimum for the second and third stories.
3. Street setback for the Main Street Building shall be 4 feet minimum / 8 feet maximum for the first and second stories, 20 feet minimum for the third story.
4. Setback from the mews for the Main Street Building shall be 6 feet minimum for the ground floor, 16 feet minimum for the second and third stories.
5. Hidden court shall have an open and closed sides; the side setback for the closed side shall be 0 feet minimum, the side setback fro the open side shall be 16 feet to the porch, 24 feet to the building.

ted on lots for each of the building types. This is an effective way to control the density in the business row. Again, these maximums are provided as a reference; the real numbers should be adjusted by either the business row organizations or the village managements. If we were to use floor area ratio[2] for density comparison, the listed total floor area maximums indicate densities between 0.8 and 1.4, which, we believe, is the appropriate density range for the business row.

The uses that business rows accommodate are light industry, office, and retail, as well as residential. Even though the size and character of the dwellings vary depending on the building type (ranging from small studios to larger apartments and townhomes), these building types indicate an average residential density of 15–20 units per acre. The residential density in the business row may be reduced if there is more demand for flex spaces where manufacturing use is predominant. It is, however, important to include a certain level of residential density within the business row to offer attainable living options for potential young or transitionary members of the labor force. We recommend no fewer than 14 units per acre average.

In terms of light industry, some simple performance standards will be needed to create a harmonious coexistence with the residential and commercial uses. We suggest this definition for light industry:

- **Light industry:** Any kind of scientific research or manufacture, compounding, assembling, processing or treatment of products, and office and office/warehouse use, provided the following limitations are placed: (a) light industry shall be operated entirely within a completely enclosed structure; (b) dust, fumes, odors, refuse matter, smoke, vapor, direct light, and vibrations generated by light industry shall be confined to the structure where such use is located; (c) noise generated by the use shall not exceed 65 dB measured along the lot boundaries, and noise levels more than 40 dB shall be limited to daylight hours; and (d) outdoor storage, equipment, and refuse areas shall be concealed from view from abutting rights-of-way.

In addition to the performance standards listed within this definition, the maximum building sizes listed on Table A.3 also indicate significant limitations to the light industry use within the business row. The table suggests a 5,000 square feet maximum for any business. Even though this is provided as a reference point and should be adjusted depending on the context, we believe that it is a reasonable size that can accommodate a large range of businesses. It becomes harder to mitigate the negative effects of even a light industry when its size gets bigger.

Support Districts

As discussed in Chapter 3, the support areas include energy and food farms, as well as recycling and waste management facilities. The character and the intensity of these facilities will be determined by the available technologies and resources where the adaptation village is located. As such, we do not have any specific density or use restriction recommendations for the support areas.

Form

The following is a select set of regulatory tools crafted to regulate the lot layouts and building forms in the adaptation village. Although by no means comprehensive, these tools can inspire and guide crafting of a comprehensive development code in any context. Here again, we will follow the order of the primary components of the adaptation village.

Neighborhoods

The design principles for blocks and successful compounds are discussed in Chapter 7. Here we focus on some lot types we have crafted following these design principles. These lot types can easily be plugged into any development code. A lot type is a set of bulk, density, and intensity regulations that are based on a specific building type. Bulk regulations define the shape of the three-dimensional envelope within which the building is permitted to be contained. Setbacks and height restrictions are the most common of the bulk regulations. Density refers to the amount of building (usually measured by floor area) that is built or is allowed to be built on a lot. As mentioned above, Tables A.1 and A.2 address the densities appropriate for compounds of different sizes in different transects. Intensity, as differentiated from density, refers to the effect of the building. Some buildings may be very intense and look too big, too oppressive; other buildings may appear cozy, modest, and friendly. Intensity is closely related to the massing articulation as well as building components that can, for instance, scale down the perceived mass.

These components usually include porches, arcades, balconies, and garden walls, which work best when employed thoughtfully as part of the building's massing articulation. The final element of a lot type is the name it is given. The name can yield important clues about the building type on which the lot type is based. For instance, a South West compound lot type, which is one of the lot types we are about to review, implies by its name a compound in a region with a hot-arid climate.

The adaptation village plans and visuals we have presented thus far assume a location close to Denver, Colorado, in a region with a temperate climate. Thus, all the compound plans and images reflect building form decisions that work for the temperate climate of Colorado's Front Range. These decisions are summarized by the Front Range compound lot type (Figure 7.26). As mentioned before, the compound plans need to be revised for different climate zones. Chapter 7 introduced two exemplary lot types for hot-arid and hot-humid climate zones: the South West compound lot type (Figure 7.27) and Southern compound lot type (Figure 7.28). Here, we review the specific regulatory measures employed by these lot types.

The first of the regulatory tools that make the Front Range compound lot type is a set of setback requirements (see the table in Figure 7.26). Let us first introduce a general definition for the term "setbacks." This definition also includes some rules of measurement:

- **Setbacks**: setbacks shall be applied as listed per each building form type following these general provisions. (a) All setbacks shall be measured from the property line to the outside of the building framing. Sheathing, drywall, siding, masonry, and insulation materials are permitted to encroach into the setbacks up to 6 inches. (b) Eaves, rakes, chimneys, scuppers, light fixtures, and similar appurtenances on the building face are permitted to encroach into the setback up to 24 inches. (c) When setbacks for various structures and building elements are not listed separately, the setback shall be applied to all structures on the lot. (d) When a maximum and a minimum are stated, the exterior building wall shall be placed in between.

Creating secure yet inviting façades for the compounds is especially important for the façades facing central common greens and green fingers. The

Front Range compound lot type addresses this with an 8-foot setback to buildings and garden walls (see, for instance, note 1 on Figure 7.26) and a zero setback to the porches and balconies. These setbacks, together with the porch or balcony requirement (see note 3), encourage, and to a degree guarantee, formation of a façade composition that is not too flat and monotonous, but instead one that provides interest for pedestrians. In addition to these measures, the green finger setbacks permit buildings to be placed on the property line with no setback along 25 percent of the frontage, which adds more articulation and break to the façade. Finally, the 30-percent eye-level transparency requirement for the tall garden walls (see note 2) adds yet another element to make these façades more inviting and friendly. Here are the definitions for garden fences and walls and eye-level transparency:

- **Garden fences and walls (short and tall)**: all fences and walls that are visible from the surrounding rights-of-way (including common greens) and located within 12 feet of the property line, are considered as garden fences or walls. All fences 42 inches high or higher are considered to be tall; all others are considered to be short. No garden fence or wall is permitted to be higher than 8 feet. (This height should be increased in hot-arid climate zones.)
- **Eye-level transparency**: Eye-level transparency is the percentage of the transparent part of the tall fences and walls (grilled openings, glazed windows, or simple openings with no barriers) in relation to the rest of the wall surface, measured within the 3-feet-wide zone that lies between 4-feet-high and 7-feet-high lines on the tall fence and wall.

For the mews-facing compound façade, there is an 8-foot setback to the building, but no setback to the balconies. Again, this, together with the porch or balcony requirement, guarantees the presence of some second-story balconies watching over the mews. Together with occasional store windows, this configuration creates a balanced coexistence of garage doors and pedestrian life on the mews.

Regarding building height, the lot types list the maximum permitted height in terms of both the number of stories and feet. Specifying the number of stories is a simple, common-sense measure. It takes away the pressure of forcing an extra story within an envelope, which usually leads to an awkward building design and happens when builders try to maximize the building floor area. Measuring the height in number of stories and assigning larger height maximums in feet encourages, or at least does not penalize, steep gable and hip roofs. Even though we all understand what a story is, defining it may be cumbersome. Here is a suggested definition along with a few rules of measurement for building height:

- **Building height**: building height shall be measured both in terms of the number of stories and the distance (in feet) from the natural grade to the highest point in the building. Building height as a distance (in feet) shall be measured following the natural terrain within the building footprint. The allowed building envelope will be defined by projecting the terrain from the ground a distance equal to the maximum height allowed. When height is measured as the number of stories, a story is defined as a floor-to-floor measurement not to exceed 12 feet, except for non-residential stories, which shall not exceed 14 feet. Single-story non-residential spaces are permitted to exceed the 14-feet limitation. Where vaulted ceilings are provided, the height measurement shall be taken at the midpoint of the main ceiling slope. If the main level is located more than 4 feet above the average grade, measured at the edges of the building footprint with basement, the level below shall be considered a story.

All compound lot types included here state a maximum height of two stories. Only a few of the lot types within the business row permit third stories. For an urbanist, this may seem to be too low as it excludes many impressive examples of successful urban architecture. However, since our purpose is to find a sweet spot in terms of the right density for achieving self-sufficiency within the walking shed, we believe that low-rise buildings offer the resilience that we need. We also believe that there is a way to create urbanity and to design strong urban spaces with low-rise buildings. Nevertheless, the number of stories should be increased in more severe hot-arid and especially hot-humid climate zones. After all, the densities as well as the number of stories we suggest here are reference points. As discussed before, depending on the context of the adaptation village, higher densities may be employed, with the caveat that this will likely reduce the level of self-sufficiency.

The next regulatory tool presented by the lot types is the lot coverage, which is an important measure that, when used thoughtfully, can encourage the right building configuration for the right climate. Here are the definitions for lot coverage and building footprint:

- **Lot coverage**: lot coverage is the percentage of the building footprint in relation to the lot area. A larger lot coverage indicates building footprints covering a larger portion of the lot.
- **Building footprint**: the building footprint is the total square footage located between and including the foundation walls of all structures on all ground floors on a lot, including garages. Covered porches, colonnades, carports, breezeways, roof overhangs, stoops, exterior stairs, and balconies shall not be included in the building footprint calculation.

Now let us focus on the two compound lot types crafted to respond to the hot-arid and hot-humid climates, namely the South West compound (Figure 7.27) and Southern compound (Figure 7.28) lot types. We have already discussed the general design principles that shaped these two lot types in Chapter 7. Here, we will briefly review the regulatory tools employed in crafting of these lot types. As mentioned before, in hot climates, the size of the court needs to get smaller as the climatic conditions grow more severe, much like a camera's diaphragm that controls the shutter aperture: the greater the amount of light, the smaller the aperture (see the cross sections provided in Figures 7.29 and 7.30). In order to reduce the size of the central courtyard, both lot types require deeper setbacks on the green finger and central common green frontages (24 feet minimum along a third of the frontage). This results in the formation of secondary courtyards along these frontages. In order for these secondary courtyards to function well, both lot types permit the garden walls and fences to be placed on the property line.

As attached buildings and increased lot coverage are desirable in hot-arid climates, the South West compound lot type permits the buildings to be placed on the side property line that is shared with the neighboring lot (so that the building may be attached to the building on the neighboring lot). Also, the lot coverage maximum is increased to allow and encourage larger ground floors and smaller second stories, which is the desired building form in hot-arid climates.

The Southern compound lot type introduces two coverage measures: a ground floor footprint that is stated as a maximum and a roof coverage that is stated as a minimum.

- **Roof coverage:** The roof coverage refers to the percentage of the area on the ground that is not directly open to the sky in relation to the lot area. Larger roof coverage indicates that a larger portion of the lot is shaded.

The hatched area on the lot diagram in Figure 7.28 indicates areas that are not directly open to the sky. As seen in this diagram, the areas directly open to the sky are very limited. The smaller ground floor footprint and larger roof coverage generate a building form that looks like an upside-down wedding cake. Limiting the size of each footprint (see note 1) encourages the formation of breezeways, especially on the ground floors, which is, as discussed earlier, desirable in hot-humid climates.

The compound lot type regulations presented thus far assume the full 120 × 120 feet lot size. Further lot types need to be crafted to address smaller lot sizes, a task to be explored in another volume. Here, we need to be brief; our purpose is to provide enough material to inspire and encourage coding the compounds according to the climatic conditions. Also, let us remind again, the measures provided here should be seen as reference points; they need to be adjusted and calibrated according to the specific climate and terrain of each region. After all, each location has its own unique conditions.

Village Center

The foreground civic buildings in the village center are unique and should be designed by discretionary review to address their particular locations and purposes. Therefore, here we will focus only on the form of the buildings on the business row. As discussed before, we propose four building types for the business row (for a reminder, see Figure 3.11). Table A.3 is a summary of the rules that make up the lot types for these buildings. Let us briefly review some of these measures. As some outdoor space may be needed for staging exhibits, a deeper street setback is assigned to the flex space buildings (12 feet minimum, 15 feet maximum), as opposed to the shallower street setbacks of the three other building types (4 feet minimum, 8 feet maximum). Note also that the upper story setbacks differ from the ground floor street setbacks listed for the hidden court, live-above, and main street building types (see notes 1–3 in Table A.3). Another regulatory tool, which is unique to the hidden court, is the introduction of open and closed sides with different setbacks, a tool employed so that the townhouses located behind the front building can face small courtyards (see note 5). Altogether, these lot types create a business row that is diverse in building form with interesting street frontages. They encourage and accommodate a wide variety of businesses, activities, and life styles.

Support Districts

The character and intensity of the facilities in the support areas will be determined by the available technologies and resources where the adaptation village will be implemented. As such, we do not have any specific form restriction recommendations for the support districts.

What we have provided here is a starting point for crafting a dynamic development code that can inspire the establishment of a healthy regulation culture for adaptation villages. These tools provide a regulatory framework that can enable a dynamic culture. Let us all hope that we will be able to observe, in the near future, the formation of adaptation villages, together with their exemplary regulation cultures and evolving development codes.

Notes

1   For this approach, please see *SmartCode*, developed by Duany Plater-Zyberk & Company, which is an open source, transect-based, unified land development ordinance template designed to create walkable neighborhoods across the full spectrum of human settlement. The code can be retrieved from https://transect.org/codes.html. See also Onaran (2019).

2   Floor area ratio is the ratio of the total building floor area accommodated on a lot in relation to the lot size. As it doesn't define the form, size, or scale of the building, it is not recommended as a regulatory tool for the adaptation village. It is referred to here only for comparison purposes.

APPENDIX B
ESSENTIAL TERMS AND CONCEPTS FOR ADAPTATION URBANISM

This appendix explores certain terms that are either used in this book or are closely related to its subject. It not only provides brief definitions of the terms, but also discusses their meanings and significance within the specific context of adaptation urbanism. As some of the terms have a diverse set of connotations that evolved in different disciplines, it is important to clarify and specify their meanings within the conceptual framework presented in this book. Some of the terms have already been discussed within the chapters of this book. However, in order not to disturb the flow, these discussions were brief. Thus there emerged the need for further discussion. This appendix provides further exploration of what is skipped and not mentioned within the chapters. Some repetition is inevitable, especially as this appendix is crafted not just as a supplement but also to be a stand-alone reference source. Also, it is by no means meant to be a comprehensive glossary. There is always more room for further exploration, which needs to be continued in upcoming volumes.

Appropriate Technology

The etymology of the word technology highlights two Greek words: *techne* means "making," and it was used for art, craft, and skill; *logos* means "words, or discourse, or knowledge." In short, technology is the knowledge of making, which points to something different than the contemporary lay use of the term, which usually refers to gadgets, machines, and electronics.

The transformation of the meaning from knowledge (tacit as in skill, or otherwise) to a black box (such as our smartphones) – where we, most users, have no knowledge of how it works – reflects another transformation that is more social in nature and that happened starting with the Industrial Revolution. As the knowledge of making became more and more complex, it was monopolized by large investors and distanced more and more from lay people. This process is the result of capitalist markets; technology, the knowledge of making, became a commodity owned by a few who controlled the means of production. The recent history of computer technology, characterized by many as "high technology," followed the same process of monopolization, but took it to an extreme. Today the "knowledge of making" a social media platform such as Facebook, used globally, belongs to a single company and can be managed and controlled only by this company, even though the platform itself has significant transformative social impacts in many societies around the globe. This is the reason why the term "high-tech" usually implies regional and global interventions. The idea that a lay person, a local, may possess the knowledge of making complicated electronic gadgets and computers is somehow foreign to most of us. However, as we reviewed in Chapter 5, there are many examples of locals successfully engaged in making complicated gadgets in places where global networks could not reach, places such as various regions of Africa. These examples tell us that the monopolization process can be reversed by diligent actors, most of the time acting out of necessity. Within the framework of adaptation, this is where we need to be: we need to figure out how to localize high technology.

The monopolization of complicated technology, also known as high-tech, puts us in a very vulnerable place in the face of possible future system failures. Especially recently, living with a pandemic, most of us have been depending heavily on social media platforms, as well as communication programs (such as Zoom, Go to Meeting, WebEx, etc.), to run our businesses and maintain our social lives. Recent power outages in Texas reminded us how vulnerable we are now, compared with where we were just 30 years ago, when we did not depend on these virtual social platforms and communication means. This does not mean that we need to reject these technologies to be more resilient; but rather we need to localize the knowledge. We need to be able to work them ourselves so that, when the large power networks go down, we may continue building using them.

In the framework of adaptation, appropriate technology is the localized knowledge of making. Fleming suggests four criteria for appropriate technology:

1. *It is accessible* – that is, affordable: it does not burden the community with debt.
2. *It is small* – that is, it does not require levels of energy, materials or a market on a scale greater than the community can supply.
3. *It has the simplicity* needed for local people to maintain and, ideally, build it themselves, using their own skills and resources.
4. *It is non-violent* in three senses: It does not make bigger demands (in terms of raw materials or pollution) than the local environment can support. It does not come at the cost of people's mental and physical health. And it does not start a sequence of damage and repair, with clean-up commitments, repairs and costs extending into the future.

(Fleming 2016a, p. 11)

As suggested in this book, this implies a paradigm shift in the fields of engineering and computer science. It is a necessary paradigm shift that will provide us with more resilience in the remainder of this difficult century and beyond.

For further exploration of the term, please see *Low Tech Magazine* at www.lowtechmagazine.com/ and *Solar Low Tech Magazine* at https://solar.lowtechmagazine.com/. See also Fleming (2016a), Hopkins (2008), Lengen (2008).

Authenticity

Even though it has not been discussed in this book thus far, authenticity is an important concept, holding various implications that allow one more easily to grasp and assess life in the adaptation village. It is a multidimensional concept with various definitions and interpretations. Authenticity (a) may be attributed to objects (art pieces, products, instruments, etc.), (b) may be constructed, or (c) may refer to our experiences.

Let us expand on these different uses of the term. The authenticity of an object refers to whether or not the object is original. This is also called museum authenticity, as we expect each artifact included in a museum to be the original. Constructed authenticity, a term Wang (1999) has introduced, refers not to the object but to the representation and the story, such as, for example, a prehistoric dwelling space reconstructed in a museum hall to represent how our distant ancestors lived. Here the term refers to the accuracy of the available archeological evidence. Theater, motion picture, and performing arts also reconstruct the past. However, in these, authenticity doesn't refer only to the accuracy of the representation, but also to the originality of the storytelling, of the artwork.

The last interpretation, the authenticity of our experiences, is the one that has the most significant implications within the framework of adaptation urbanism. Authenticity of a meaningful experience implies a state of being in which one is true to oneself. An authentic experience, as opposed to a shallow experience, is unique, valuable, and worthwhile – it is real, not fake. It goes hand in hand with contentment and happiness, both of which motivate us to be social and engaged in communal activities. Chambers (2000), in exploring the concept from an anthropological view, states:

> my sense of authentic is that it occurs under conditions in which people have significant control over their affairs, to the extent that they are able to play an active role in determining how changes occur in their social settings.
>
> (p. 98)

This relationship between autonomy and authentic experience is important for us. Only when we (as an individual or as a community) have control over the factors shaping our daily lives and participate in making decisions regarding how we live can we consider our experiences as uniquely ours and meaningful. Only with certain amount of autonomy can we be true to ourselves.

Within the framework of the adaptation village, coordination and management at compound, block, and walking shed scales, organized following the subsidiarity principle, are important steps towards achieving enough autonomy and having meaningful authentic experiences. Furthermore, at a more personal level, diversifying our means of earning our bread and having control over our weekly schedules and agility in working and living close by or even on the same lot – all of which are offered by the compound model in the adaptation village – contribute to our autonomy and enable our experiences to be unique and special. This is an important attribute of the daily life in an adaptation village as we envision it: authentic experience, both individually and as a community.

For further exploration of the term, please see Wang (1999) and Chambers (2000). We also recommend Knudsen and Waade (2010).

Calibration

Calibration refers to adjustment. It has a strong affinity with the term adaptation. It suggests an evolving life adjusting to ever-changing conditions, as opposed to stability and rigidness. As such it is, and needs to be, an integral part of designing, planning, and managing adaptation villages. We need to calibrate to adapt to a new reality. This implies agility and requires monitoring ever-changing conditions and being realistic about our expectations.

Following the adaptation framework introduced in this book, there are three calibration categories: sustenance systems, governance and social organization, and the design of the physical environment. Localization of sustenance systems is enabled by nesting. This means production at the higher scales needs to be calibrated according to production at the lower scales (compound and block scales). The systems need to be calibrated according to the available sources of the context. The same principle applies for governance and social order. Subsidiarity, along with the prerequisites of sharing, giving, and enjoyment, are the goals for which ownership and governance need to be calibrated. This calibration needs to take into account the amount and character of shared amenities (including energy farms, water storage, greenhouses, recycling facilities, etc.). Furthermore, an ownership and governance model may work in one political landscape in one location, but may need to be recalibrated for the next. As noted, the site plan layout, densities, and the amount of land to be reserved for support services in adaptation villages and districts will depend on the context and the types of available technologies. The design principles introduced in this book (nesting, transect, succession, gathering, secure place, and climate-conscious design) are the goals with which all the design measures and decisions need to be calibrated.

For further exploration of the term, please see Duany and Steuteville (2021), and Fleming (2016a).

Climacteric

Climacteric refers to periods of profound change in the life of a system, such as marriage, migration, or a job change in the life of a person. Some theories suggest that these stages happen every 7 years in someone's life. Fleming (2016a) uses the term to emphasize the drastic change life on the planet will experience in the period between 2010 and 2040, a decade of which we have already lived through as of the writing of this book. He argues that the climacterics for human society could include the end of the last ice age, the start of agricultural society, and the Industrial Revolution. The change that will be experienced within the period between 2010 and 2040 is the next stage. Climate change and steep increases in the human population challenge the current economic system, which depends on growth at all costs, despite operating within a global system that has finite resources. Shortages of energy, water, food, and other natural resources will result in severe disruptions of the social, economic, and ecological order.

One of the premises of this book is that the shock is inevitable; therefore, rather than asking how to prevent it, the focus needs to be on the question of how to develop the skills and resources to "build the resilient sequel to our present society" (Fleming, 2016a, p. 45). Fleming (2016a) echoes the primary assumptions of this book and depicts a future that is consistent with the general adaptation framework of this book. He claims that the lean society

> will be the decentralized, low-impact human ecology which has always taken the human story forward from the closing down of civilizations: small-scale, community, closed-loop systems, and a strong culture.
>
> (p. 45)

For further exploration of the term, please see Fleming (2016a, 2016b).

Comfort Zone

Comfort zone refers to places where human comfort is achieved in terms of the right temperature, air quality, and humidity. The principle of climate-conscious design refers to creating comfort zones without depending on advanced mechanical heating and cooling machinery, but employing the right site layout, building form, and material.

Throughout the history of human settlements, creating comfort zones has been a challenge, especially in regions with severe climate conditions. Even though we depend mostly on advanced mechanical heating and cooling machinery to sustain comfort zones nowadays, this was not an option until quite recently. Consequently, previous generations have created a rich set of architectural archetypes, building forms, and technologies that created comfort zones without the help of advanced machinery. Learning from these precedents is one key to increasing resilience. Sustaining life in buildings designed without paying attention to the climatic conditions usually depends on heavy energy consumption. The tougher the climate, the higher the energy consumption! High levels of consumption are becoming increasingly problematic, especially in hot regions. As yearly average temperatures are increasing all around the globe, the regions with hot climates are expanding. In recent years, we have observed life-threatening heat waves. When coinciding with power shortages, heat waves can be fatal, especially where the built environment is not shaped to create comfort zones naturally. Furthermore, dependence on advanced mechanical heating and cooling machinery, especially in extreme climates, forces the public realm and places for gathering to be confined to air-conditioned interior spaces, which reduces casual neighborly interaction. Meaningful neighborly interaction and the richness of social life are prerequisites for enabling sharing and giving and sustaining governance of the localization of sustenance systems.

There are many good sources that review building archetypes where comfort zones have been created by design. These include: Onaran (2019), Nikeghbali (2017), Konya and Vandenberg (2011), Givoni (1998), Hakim (1988), and Fathy (1986). From these can be gleaned a few general design principles for hot-arid and hot-humid climates. The temperature difference between day and night increases as the level of humidity in the air decreases. In dry regions, there are significant temperature changes not only between the day and night, but also between surfaces exposed to the sun and those that are not. In the vernacular architecture of hot-arid climate zones, we usually observe that buildings are attached to each other and face small courtyards. Streets are narrow. In other words, the courtyards and narrow streets are the only outdoor spaces, and they are limited: most of the ground is covered by buildings. Buildings open only to the courtyards and don't have any other façades exposed to the sun. In hot-arid climates, unshaded paved areas can create heat islands easily. Providing tall, narrow courtyards (where

the width is smaller than the height) is the most effective way to create a
shaded area with its own micro-climate. The courtyards may get a bit wider
in regions where large canopy trees are feasible (such as semi-arid regions
and regions with highland climates and semi-dry winters). However, in arid
desert regions, the courtyard proportions become the most important factor
in providing shade. Another principle of hot-arid urbanism is to cover most
of the ground with buildings, but provide less floor area on the upper floors
to catch the evening breezes. This creates a building form that looks like a
wedding cake. In terms of the breezes in hot-arid regions, air movement
should be blocked during the day so that the shaded micro-climates (such
as those created in courtyards) are protected and not exposed to hot air. In
the evening, however, when the air cools down, air movement should be
maximized to allow the cool air to flow into the courtyards and interior
spaces.

In hot-humid climates, humidity holds the heat close to the ground and
doesn't allow surfaces to emit the heat back to the sky in the evening. When
there is humidity in the air, the sun reaches and heats up the ground at a
slower rate, but, once heated, the surfaces cannot cool down easily because
the humidity holds the heat. The only way to cool heated areas then is
to move the air, that is, to create breezes. As in the hot-arid regions, creating shade in hot-humid regions is essential for creating comfort, but is
not enough in itself; air movement needs to be created. As it is so hard to
cool down surfaces once heated, creating shade is much more important for
hot-humid climates. Preventing surfaces from heating up in the first place
is essential. Careful landscaping and shaded water features are two means
used for cooling down the air. However, it is air movement that maximizes
any such cooling effect. All these characteristics suggest urban design principles that are opposite to what we have reviewed for the hot-arid regions.
Instead of attaching buildings and creating large footprints on the ground
floor, detaching buildings from each other and minimizing ground-floor
footprints of buildings should be the strategy. Detaching buildings from
each other, with narrow distances in between, helps to move the air; such
spaces can work as breeze funnels and create breezeways. Buildings close
to each other with large overhangs create shade and air movement. In hot-
humid regions, buildings with limited ground-floor footprints and larger
upper floors are desirable, as opposed to buildings with large footprints.
This means turning the "wedding cake" upside down. Maze-like hollow

buildings touching the ground in limited ways, organized under large roofs, are ideal. Rather than sitting on grade, having ventilation under the slab via crawl spaces is also helpful. In hot-humid climate regions, buildings raised on stilts are common. In urban contexts, where stilts may not be practical, having limited ground floors with most of the floor area located on the upper floors is an effective way to ventilate the underside of the upper floors. Simple roof shapes with large overhangs are desirable not only because they work better for heavy rainfall, but also because they expose the least amount of building massing to the sun. Ventilating the attics and crawlspaces is a must. Materials such as stucco and mudbrick that keep the heat are not preferrable in hot-humid climates, but rather materials that reflect the sun radiation and don't hold the heat should be employed. Lighter building materials with no insulation are typical because, unless mechanically cooled, enclosed spaces with no air movement are almost impossible to cool in natural ways. As a matter of fact, in extreme humid climates, the demarcation between the interior and the exterior preferably disappears.

These are general principles. There are unique climatic variations with various nuances in each specific location on our globe. This makes it necessary to revisit these general design principles and to adjust the building form in order to create comfort zones naturally in each specific location.

For further exploration of the term, please see Fathy (1986), Givoni (1998), Konya and Vandenberg, (2011), and Onaran (2019).

Compound

The term compound refers to a group of buildings clustered to create a meaningful relationship with each other. Within the framework of the adaptation village, these buildings are located on a single lot, owned by a single owner – a person, a family, or, occasionally, a small homeowners' association (HOA). A central courtyard where residents of the compound gather and socialize is also an important component of the archetype within the framework of adaptation urbanism. The compound development model enables gradual growth and succession.

In addition to residential use, a compound in the adaptation village accommodates light industry, retail, and farming on a modest scale. The compound model provides financial resilience for the households because it allows productive activities on the lot and it enables gradual growth by the addition of one structure at a time. Compounds offer rental dwelling units and rental business spaces that are crucial in accommodating a workforce with diverse demographics within the adaptation village. Furthermore, the compound model offers an opportunity to create a social pod, which encourages residents to see their neighbors not as competitors but as valuable amenities.

Unlike the terms "cluster" and "group," compound implies a whole formed by necessary and contributing parts; each part has an essential role in defining the character of the whole. In spite of the defense-related connotations of the term (complexes that are walled or fenced for protection), compound fits into the framework of adaptation because it suggests synergies between the elements that form the compound, which is a prerequisite for self-sufficiency and resilience. Thus, there is a level of self-sufficiency as well as symbiosis implied by the term compound. This implication fits well with the concept of hybrid land use; each building forming the compound accommodates an activity or use that supports and forms the life of the compound and makes it a whole.

For further exploration of the term, please see Markham (2012), Polyzoides, Sherwood, and Tice (1992), and Volk (2017).

Defensible Space

Defensible space, a term introduced by Oscar Newman with his book *Defensible Space* (1976), refers to enhancing security within a territory by means of the layout of the space as well as the activities surrounding it. There is a level of security that can be provided without active policing or specialized security measures, but instead relying on "eyes on the street," a term introduced by Jane Jacobs (1961). The strength of the social ties and the layout of the gathering places can be instrumental in creating and sustaining a secure place. If there is a strong sense of ownership over a social space (for instance, if many of the residents know each other and use the space regularly), and if the layout of the space allows residents and business owners to see and observe the space easily, then the setting tends to be relatively safe. Certain archetypes, such as common greens, compounds, blocks, perimeter blocks, and perimeter courtyard clusters create defensible space that supports rather than rejects social life. The key in defensible space is the residents' ability (enabled by the spatial layout) to transform "strangers" into "acquaintances" or "friends" by means of social interaction. A porch located close to a sidewalk, for instance, encourages a pedestrian to acknowledge the person sitting on the porch. If the acknowledgment turns into a brief exchange, the stranger is transformed into an acquaintance. This is also an important step towards creating a social order of trust, care, and support.

For further exploration of the term, please see Cisneros (1995), Crowe and Fennelly (2012), and Office of Community Oriented Policing Services (COPS), U. S. Department of Justice (2012).

Ecology

The origin of the term goes back to the Greek *oikos*, meaning home, or household, and *logos*, meaning "word, or discourse, or knowledge." Used for the first time by the German zoologist Ernst Haeckel (1834–1919), the term *oekologie* referred to the study of a habitat as it is transformed by various species. It was a new way of understanding the interactions between the species and their environments, their habitats; the interactions between the species' lives, needs, consumptions, and the life-sustaining resources of their habitat, as well as other environmental factors such as geography, topography, and climate.

In time, since it exposed, in a wholistic way, environmental destruction caused by our Western consumption patterns, ecology challenged mainstream lifestyles and created a new paradigm for living: finding ways to survive without creating imbalances in ecosystems – light living with limited impact. This paradigm gave way to the grass-roots environmentalism of the 1960s and created strong opposition to unlimited use of natural resources and resource extraction. It also pushed many to question their consumption patterns and search for alternative lifestyles. Around that time, the term "eco" was transformed as a prefix to mean anything that is environment-friendly, as in eco-home, eco-district, eco-city, and so forth.

Within the framework of adaptation, it is helpful to remember the root meaning – the knowledge of home, or community, if we expand the meaning of home. As such, the term is closely related to equilibrium, as the ultimate practical purpose of this knowledge is to create balance between many competing influences and forces within a community and its use of resources and means of production. This affinity between ecology and equilibrium fits well with this book's "action framework of adaptation" that highlights "equilibrium in localization" and our overarching objective.

Enjoyment

Within the framework of adaptation urbanism, enjoyment is one of the three prerequisites for achieving a social order where the residents are motivated to participate in social life, production, and management of the localized sustenance systems. The other two are giving and sharing. If the life depicted in the adaptation village is to come to be, and to be sustained, it must be enjoyable. For many of us, this will require a paradigm shift in what we find enjoyable. We need to treat the subject of enjoyment seriously. Usually, it is our own frame of mind – our own work ethic – that prevents our enjoyment; no matter how rigorously we pursue it, the voice in our mind tells us that our enjoyment is not deserved or earned. This widespread work ethic forces us to see anything but worthwhile production as a waste of time, that spending our time with our neighbors is time not worthwhile, not well lived, and that our community engagement is only an obligation, not enjoyment. Anything fun is a "guilty pleasure" to be regretted immediately after.

The Protestant work ethic that underlined "guilty pleasure" gave way to the kind of production processes that created capitalism and became widespread in the West. We rationalized and systematized our activities of production and developed tools to monitor how we use our time at work. Nowadays, it is common to work 40–50 hours a week or more, at a remote workplace away from home, with long, grueling commutes. We brag about how little sleep we need. Many workers come to feel like they are part of a machine run by a distant authority beyond reach. And, for some who work in large manufacturing factories, this is literally the case, as Charlie Chaplin so eloquently pointed out in his movie *Modern Times*.

This kind of life is neither balanced nor resilient. It is surely not enjoyable either. If and when we lose our jobs, suddenly life becomes very difficult. We have put all of our eggs in one basket, and the fate of our work is controlled by others. Even if we own our own business, the fate of the business may depend on larger-scale factors that are beyond our control, which was the case for many restaurant owners especially in the early months of the lockdown due to the pandemic. So, how do we increase resilience in our daily lives regarding our work? How do we have energy left over to spend time with our family, neighbors, and friends, to get involved in local activities and management that affect enjoyment and quality of life?

The financial meltdown of 2008 and the COVID-19 pandemic give us some hints. Similar to our argument for strengthening local economies, one answer is to diversify what we do and to do it in a way to reduce dependence. Many businesses have already learned the importance of being small, agile, and maintaining limited overheads. After the meltdown of 2008, some large firms shrank, and many small offices were formed by those who had lost their jobs. We also learned that we could live with working fewer hours, or at a different pace, or doing things we loved. Some started their own businesses on the side, either in the field they had been working in or by diversifying their interests and forming a creative mixture of services. These are important lessons for how we can create a more localized and independent business landscape for the future, as well as how we can put aside more time in order to be a part of local governance. This kind of landscape, especially if created collectively, as we hope to see in adaptation villages, can create a resilient or lean local economy where the time spent on communal activities can not only be enjoyable but also actually pay back and support the household budget significantly.

Working-from-home is another important transformation we have experienced during lockdown. Many of us realized that running a business from home is possible. In spite of its disadvantages, it reclaims time from commuting and provides more autonomy about how we organize our workspace, which has enabled us to diversify our work endeavors. This transformation provides important clues about the social order in an adaptation village, where we expect residents to devote time to involvement in local governance and management. It also underlines the necessity of the hybrid nature of a compound where the separation and the distance between home and various forms of work are minimized.

To move our discussion back to the term enjoyment, "the guilty pleasure," the antithesis of enjoyment, has another important consequence: it distances us from the decision-making processes that affect our lives; it forces us to act in an anti-democratic way. In his book *Terra Madre*, Carlo Petrini, the founder of the Slow Food movement, states:

> Pleasure is democratic. … Pleasure is democratic because it makes us want to become active players again, even if this only means performing small acts to improve our daily lives. The pleasure of eating is potentially the most immediate and the most accessible pleasure for all of us. And eating pleasurably may be a disruptive political act. Pleasure is not elitist; it is a right that needs to be protected, promoted, and enjoyed by all.
>
> (Petrini, 2009, p. 51)

Enjoying pleasures in life, even the simple ones such as eating, is a way of developing preferences, which is a prerequisite for any democratic debate. Without any preferences, our vote becomes a blind vote. Enjoyment (and having preferences) is not just butter on bread, but it is the bread itself. It is not only a healthy way of slowing down, but a civic responsibility for creating a resilient democratic order.

We can find joy in knowing even our crankiest neighbors and see them as assets. This may soon become a matter of necessity if, and when, we face isolation and desolation in the age of climate disasters. The ownership and management models we suggest for adaptation urbanism provide the framework within which neighbors are enabled to be assets for each other. But it is up to each of us to see more clearly the advantages of diversifying our endeavors and our companions and enjoy giving to, as well as taking from, our communities. It is up to each of us to face the paradigm shift we need to find enjoyment in all endeavors in our lives.

For more comprehensive discussion on the relationship between the Protestant work ethic and the rationalization and systematization of the production process, see Max Weber's (1906) *The Protestant Ethic and Spirit of Capitalism*. Also, especially for the effect of this rationalization and systematization on our territorial control strategies, please refer to David R. Sack's (1986) book *Human Territoriality: Its theory and history*. For the consequences of overworking and commuting for long hours, see Charles Montgomery's (2013) *Happy City*.

Gift Economy

In his book *Talking to My Daughter about the Economy*, Yannis Varoufakis (2017), the former finance minister of Greece, provides an interesting story where he quotes Richard Radford, the British economist, who spent time in a prisoner-of-war camp as a captured British soldier during World War II. Using Radford's experience, Varoufakis explains to his young daughter basic economic terms such as arbitrage, deflation, inflation, exchange value, and experiential value via what went on in the closed market created by the soldiers in the camp. Soldiers received packages from the Red Cross periodically that included a few necessities – soap, toothpaste, food, and so on – as well as a few modest luxury items such as cigarettes, tea, coffee, and chocolate. Exchanges started between the tea-loving British soldiers and coffee-loving French soldiers. But soon the bartering became complex, and cigarettes (because of their scale and durability) became the currency to barter for other items. Some soldiers hoarded them to decrease the amount in circulation and thus increase the value of the cigarettes as currency. A stressful night with bombing nearby, where many smoked a lot of cigarettes, created deflation. The news that the war might end soon created inflation, and so on. The chapter ends with this anecdote: when Yannis shared this story with his father, who was put in a jail for political prisoners during the Greek Civil War of 1946–1949, his father's response was telling. He said: "No we didn't have any such market. We shared whatever packages each of us received. … That's how it was. We helped each other out."

This story highlights the difference between the market economy and the gift economy. It also emphasizes the importance of giving. While a market economy may maximize production and efficiency, a gift economy supports strong social ties, motivates involvement, and provides financial resilience.

For further exploration of the term, please see the Foundation for Intentional Community at www.ic.org/community-classifieds/. See also Ludwig and Gimnig (2021).

Giving

Within the framework of adaptation urbanism, giving is one of the three prerequisites for achieving a social order where the residents are motivated to participate in the social life, production, and management of localized sustenance systems. The other two are enjoyment and sharing. Giving refers to a localized philanthropy and gift economy. Donating one's labor is also an important form of giving. Giving labor has a significant community-building function. It also creates more practical interaction between neighbors; neighbors feel more motivated to work out conflicts and more tolerant of disturbances. Tolerance is a form of giving. In isolated societies with closed sustenance systems, members tend to see clearly how their lives depend on the work of others and thus tend to be more tolerant of real and perceived differences.

Many of us acquainted with philanthropy think of rich donors supporting the arts, schools, and other social institutions. Perhaps we've given money ourselves to such good causes. Or we have donated time and effort as a volunteer, made soup for a sick friend, or gave away goods we no longer had use for. Times of emergency and disaster increase our awareness of how crucial the help of others is. After such disasters, even more than in regular times, we tend to be ready and motivated to give and help others. This is a basic and admirable human trait. It can be challenging, however, to enable this help, to find ways to reach the people who need it. When conventional communities are cut off from the power grid, when roads are damaged and closed, residents are left by themselves, sometimes even for months, as we have experienced with some of the recent disasters. Jobs and income are lost. These disasters are extreme cases but are becoming more common. The conclusion is that we need to proactively localize philanthropy.

Being proactive means we plan ahead. Instead of waiting for a disaster to call on our local resources, we strengthen them now. This is one of the premises of creating receiving zones in the first place. Giving to invest in the localization of sustenance systems, and thus enabling people to move away from danger via making it an attractive choice, is better than trying to reach victims after a disaster. Investing in strengthening local social support systems is also a proactive way to be prepared. Giving doesn't need to be only from the few who are rich. Each and every one of us can give some of our wealth or time and labor to the community's common good. To be convinced, we just need to see clearly how essential such giving can be in creating a strong community and achieving resilience. Mutual aid groups, which pop up during dire times, can exist as a daily way of life.

Giving labor, especially at a local scale, has a significant community building function as well. For one thing, we usually see the gratifying results of our giving more immediately. Donating labor usually also creates more practical interaction between neighbors, and thus we end up feeling more motivated to work out conflicts. Practical interaction occurs when we see a clear objective for the interaction and this clear objective dominates, and possibly eliminates, any possible hidden motives. The discussion of what color the community house should be painted can instigate conflict of egos and create petty disagreements. But a decision about fixing the local water distribution system may be made faster as the participants can see clearly the larger necessity. Practical interactions strengthen our ties with each other and motivate us to give and invest more in community building.

Practical interactions can also help us be more tolerant of disturbances. Tolerance is a form of giving and increases with necessity. In isolated societies with closed sustenance systems, the members tend to see clearly how their lives depend on the work of others and thus tend to be more tolerant. The near future may force us to experience isolation at various scales, levels, and durations. We have already experienced isolation with the COVID-19 pandemic. Family members quarantining together learned how to be more tolerant of each other, as the alternative could be disastrous; in other families, disasters did in fact happen, which further strengthens our point.

Philanthropy has been an important part of our society and has been a strong financial force that contributed to civility. Without civility, our society tends to leave behind the weak, the troubled, and the unfortunate, which then potentially increases the risk for social disorder. Thus, philanthropy's role may become even more essential in the future when we are faced with uncertainties, irregularities, and unusual conditions. Helping and giving to each other, working on mutually beneficial projects together, is a way of building our own "social capital" or "social security" when government support is, at the very least, uncertain.

For further discussion on this subject, please see the Foundation of Intentional Communities www.ic.org/), which is an organization dedicated to sustainable and just ways of living together, via sharing, giving, and other intentional strategies.

Loose Space

Loose space, a term introduced by Karen Franck and Quentin Stevens (2007), refers to public space that is appropriated, even temporarily, by people to pursue activities not set by predetermined program. Buskers and impromptu musicians claiming plazas as their stages, protestors occupying intersections, or vendors strategically positioning their counters on a street corner are among examples where appropriation is negotiated within the public realm. There are also more subtle examples: kids playing ball games on the less travelled streets, a shop owner putting a table on the sidewalk to hang out with fellow shop owners, residents claiming the tree lawns (greens between the sidewalk and the street) to grow food, a class meeting forming a circle on the lawn in a park, and so on. Franck and Stevens state: "For a site to become loose, people themselves must recognize the possibilities inherent in it and make use of the possibilities for their own ends, facing the potential risks of doing so" (p. 2).

Even though it hasn't been highlighted thus far, loose space is an important concept within the framework of adaptation urbanism. It underlines the kind of conviviality reached through possibility, diversity, and disorder (as opposed to certainty, homogeneity, and order) and pushes the boundaries of social flexibility, tolerance, and acceptance. It highlights the public space as a place where, in spite of conflicts, ideas, expressions, and differences meet, face each other, and reconcile, which is the prerequisite for a community where members are motivated to be involved.

In order to comprehend the full picture of looseness, we need to understand why, especially in Western cities, we have ended up with overregulated, tight spaces. The kind of work ethic that systematized the way we organize our time has been mentioned above. The separation of work space away from all others has also been discussed. Today, in taut economies, monitoring activities and tight bookkeeping are part of daily life. This rationalization and systematization process affects the way we use our spaces. David Sack (1986) studies this transformation through his theory of territoriality. He defines the concept of territoriality as "the attempt by an individual or group to affect, influence, or control people, phenomena, and relationships, by delimiting and asserting control over a geographic area" (p. 19). The "no smoking" sign in a room, for instance, is a rule applied to a territory. Sack argues that, by applying control to a territory rather than to people, territorial controls have the ability to impersonalize social relations, a strategy he identifies with modernity. Impersonalization of relations is an important characteristic of bureaucracies, a mechanism that is assumed to provide uniformity and impartiality. In addition to impersonalizing social relations, territorial controls make it easy to exclude activities from territories. Sack calls this process the thinning out process, that is, making more and more places containers of just one type of activity. By not allowing any other activity in a territory but production, it becomes much easier to monitor labor; we just assume that the time spent in the production space is used for production, nothing else. Hence punch cards. The thinning out process goes hand in hand with an increasing division of labor, specialization, and organizational hierarchies. In other words, the hierarchical classification of spaces and a control system that assigns restrictions to territories become integral parts of bureaucracies and enable them to function efficiently. Territorial controls that are exercised by governments and other institutions to impersonalize relations and to systematize activities imply a regulation culture that is highly formal and technocratic, as opposed to the dynamic regulation culture that we suggest for the adaptation village.

The use of territorial controls by governments to distribute public services and to collect revenues is another example of a bureaucratic system.

These two mechanisms go hand in hand; for instance, once we zone certain parcels of land for retail only, then we provide utilities for "retail" use and tax these properties in the "retail" category. These mechanisms contribute significantly to formalization of the regulation culture. The emergence of zoning can be seen as a part of this formalization and thinning out process as well. These trends work against creating and sustaining a vital, inclusive, and inspiring public realm. They work against creating loose spaces as well. In their book *Sidewalks: Conflict and negotiation over public space* (2012), Loukaitou-Sideris and Ehrenfeucht review how, over time, zoning regulations have slowly excluded certain activities and certain user groups from public spaces. In Los Angeles, for instance, the city they studied in detail, for certain sidewalks this exclusion reaches a level where we start to question if we should call these places public anymore.

Conviviality and civic pride increase with discretion and looseness. They decrease and even disappear as a result of thinning out. A dynamic regulation culture that emphasizes accommodation and inclusion, as opposed to exclusion and thinning out, enables creation of loose space. This is important for the kind of conviviality that needs to be sustained within all common places in the adaptation village, but is particularly essential for the mews and business rows if we are to expect a succession of a diverse set of businesses for a strong local economy.

For further exploration of the concept and above-presented discussion, please see Franck and Stevens (2007), Fernando (2007), Dovey and Polakit (2007), Loukaitou-Sideris and Ehrenfeucht (2012), and Sack (1986).

Nesting

Nesting refers to the fitting of a shape, form, or object inside a larger one. Systems, organizations, and productions can also nest within each other. Within the framework of adaptation, nesting as a principle works on three levels: the organization of sustenance systems, the management of subsidiarity, and the physical environment. These are interdependent and support one another. In the adaptation village, a building fits within a compound, which fits within a block, which fits within a quadrant, which fits within a village, which fits within a region. The management authorities, as well as the organization of sustenance systems, follow this nesting order as well.

Nesting, in principle, enables the small. There are good reasons for a strong presumption in favor of small. The advantages of large scale can come at a high cost. Large-scale systems are vulnerable. This is especially the case considering possible system failures due to the climate crisis. Small also refers to local governance. The principle of subsidiarity is all about enabling the small but also addressing the necessity of larger-scale authorities to address issues that cannot be addressed at the local level.

Largeness may (a) lead to excessive standardization and bureaucratization, (b) reduce social consciousness and the sense of personal civic responsibility, and, thus, (c) weaken democratic processes.

Permaculture

Bill Mollison and David Holmgren (1978), two of the early advocates of permaculture, define the term as:

> The conscious design and maintenance of agriculturally productive systems which have the diversity, stability, and resilience of natural ecosystems. It is the harmonious integration of the landscape with people providing their food, energy, shelter and other material and non-material needs in a sustainable way.
>
> (p. 4)

As contrasted with today's widespread conventional, mechanized monoculture that aims to produce, with the minimum amount of labor, the largest amount of single food products to be shipped away, permaculture focuses on creating synergies between a diverse set of productive activities at a small scale to support the lives of residents and locals. It is organic and energy-efficient, but labor-intensive. It focuses on self-reliance in terms of resource conservation, especially the use of soil and water. Creating synergies and sustaining cooperation are key. Common practices entail using gentle swales bordered with water-keeping plant species to absorb each and every drop of rain that lands on the land, rather than draining it away; relying on birds and chickens to eat the bugs rather than using pesticides; and combining small greenhouses and small animal barns to create mutual support in heating. The hydroponic and aquaponic farming noted in Chapter 5 are also good examples of achieving self-sufficiency by means of synergies. Hydroponic farming is a method of growing plants without soil, instead using mineral nutrient solutions in a water solvent. Aquaponics is a form of agriculture that combines raising fish in tanks with soilless plant culture, where the nutrient-rich water from raising fish provides a natural fertilizer for the plants, while the plants help to purify the water for the fish.

Permaculture aspires to the kind of complexity observed in a mature forest. It is not just the number of species that makes a mature forest resilient, productive, and self-reliant, but the number of useful connections between these species. Patrick Whitefield (1993), in his landmark book titled *Permaculture in a Nutshell*, suggests:

> Some of the edible ecosystems of permaculture may actually look like a forest, for example a forest garden, in which fruit trees and bushes, herbs and vegetables, are all grown together, on top of each other.
>
> (p. 3)

Recently, the term permaculture has expanded beyond its essential roots of edible ecosystems and food growing practices to include societal interactions as a guiding principle for creating resilient communities. In their book titled *Human Permaculture*, Alonso and Guiochon (2020) define the term "human permaculture" in the following way:

> Human permaculture is about the interaction of human talents, together in teams, to create life in all its forms.
>
> (p. 17)

When defined in a more inclusive way, permaculture is very much in line with the concept of balanced localization and has many commonalities with the transition town movement and Transition Network (explained below). Self-reliance, diversity, and creating mutual support in between productive activities are the common principles.

We see a unique opportunity in establishing a strong relationship between permaculture, transition towns, and urbanism. The adaptation village model provides the first step. The application of the term permaculture goes beyond the food growing practices that can take place in the food farm of the adaptation village. The kind of urbanism that is structured by means of the balanced localization principles provided in this book will be able to give a community the power to achieve the self-reliance that will be very much needed to cope with the realities of the climate crisis. As the title of this book suggests, this is practical; we have a unique opportunity to create a landscape of self-sufficiencies where a network of lean economies will enable locals to be creative, productive, and motivated to support each other. This is how permaculture and adaptation urbanism can meet in facilitating balanced localization.

For further exploration of the term, please see the Permaculture Institute (https://permaculture.org/) and the Permaculture Research Institute (www.permaculturenews.org/). Also see Holmgren (2018), Markham (2012), Mollison (1988), Mollison and Holmgren (1978), Volk (2017), and Whitefield (1993).

Sharing

Within the framework of adaptation urbanism, sharing is one of the three prerequisites for achieving a social order where the residents are motivated to participate in the social life, production, and management of localized sustenance systems. The other two are enjoyment and giving. It is said that you can easily unfriend a friend on social media, but you can't un-neighbor a neighbor. How do we move away from seeing our neighbors as annoying or as competition for the sunny spot in the park – and instead see them as valuable assets who help and support many aspects of our daily lives and add to social resilience? Sharing – of space, of goods, of responsibilities – is an important first step.

One familiar social organization model, cohousing, offers important lessons. (It is one of the models we propose for the compound or block in the adaptation village.) Cohousing depends on sharing. The initial residents, usually invited and assembled by the cohousing organizer or developer before construction, decide what to share. Guestrooms, for instance, are a common shared amenity in many cohousing complexes. Instead of each unit having extra bedrooms for guests, the cohousing community builds a few guestrooms within the community house to share. Woodworking shops, art studios, common kitchens for large gatherings, landscaping tools, and storage sheds are among other popular shared amenities in cohousing projects. What these have in common is that they are quite attainable if shared, but too expensive if owned individually by each household. (Shared amenities also save space and reduce consumption.) Sometimes, these amenities are even rented to the larger community outside the cohousing community; for example, the community house may be rented out for meetings and conferences organized by others, especially in neighborhoods where such gathering spaces are rare. For example, Nomad Cohousing in Boulder, Colorado, where the majority of the initial residents were performance artists, decided to build a performance theater next to the cohousing complex, which they shared with the larger community.

Sharing becomes a more important enabler as we focus on the diversification of small-scale production. The more diverse the production, the stronger the local economy. This is very similar to the way permaculture involves a diverse set of productive activities that support each other. Within the framework of the adaptation village, a household would have difficulty producing much diversity even if it were a full-time food producer; the compound scale offers a few more opportunities. But, at the block scale, we can start talking about shared amenities such as fruit drying facilities, storage with coolers, composting facilities, small gardening machinery, and so on. Also, in terms of production, sharing increases diversity via networking and organizing among neighbors. One neighbor brings milk from her goats, the other brings eggs from his chickens, and before you know it there is enough diversity on the table, even at the block scale, for the third neighbor to start a modest bakery with only a few supplies needed from outside. The possibilities grow significantly as we move to the walking shed scale. However, all this sharing and organizing can happen only if neighbors have the desire and time to share.

For more information about cohousing, please refer to McCamant and Durrett (2011). Also see ScottHanson and ScottHanson (2004).

Succession

Succession refers to evolution towards symbiosis. It is growth with an increasing diversity of species interacting with each other in a symbiotic and mutually supportive harmony. When the term is applied to urban development as a metaphor, it refers to maturing relationships between various activities that take place in an urban neighborhood. When administrative systems enable members' agility to adopt and respond to new conditions to create stronger social ties and stronger support between productive and communal activities, the increasing complexity of social relations resembles the biodiversity of a symbiotic ecosystem.

Succession implies increasing conviviality, diversity, and richness in social interactions. It also implies a diversified local economy thriving through networking and mutual support, as well as competition. This requires a governing system and social order that enable small entrepreneurs to fill with ease the niches that emerge in the market with changing times. These niches usually correspond to much-needed support services that help communities to become financially more resilient and self-sufficient.

In terms of the development of the physical environment, succession requires agility in transformation and metamorphosis. The physical environment needs to be altered to support symbiotic relationships. Remodeling, replacing, consolidating, subdividing, reusing, repurposing, and adding are crucial building construction activities to achieve succession.

For further exploration of the term, please see Dramstad, Olson, and Forman (1996) and Lengen (2008).

Third Place

Third place, a term introduced by Oldenburg (1999), is "a generic designation for a great variety of public places that host the regular, voluntary, informal, and happily anticipated gatherings of individuals beyond the realms of home and work" (p. 16). These are coffeehouses, tea gardens, pubs, beer gardens, taverns, main streets, markets, and so on. Home is the first place, work is the second, and the third place is where we regularly go to socialize as part of our daily lives.

Oldenburg (1999) lists some characteristics as criteria to assess how successful a third place is. Successful third places are (a) neutral grounds (where anybody – the mayor as well as the construction worker – can come in); (b) levelers (where people – the mayor as well as the construction worker – talk to each other without the barriers of social status or title); (c) where people converse (meaningful social interaction is the dominant activity); (d) accessible and accommodating; (e) where there are regulars; (f) with a low profile; (g) where the mood is playful; and (h) homy and welcoming. After discussing these characteristics, Oldenburg provides a long list of personal and social benefits of third places. Among these benefits, four are especially significant within the framework of adaptation urbanism: successful third places increase social consciousness, encourage the spirit of democracy, create a communal memory, and enhance communal identity and a sense of belonging.

In order to grasp how important a role third places can play in sustaining civic involvement and responsibility, it is eye-opening to look back in history. In his book titled *A History of the World in 6 Glasses*, Standage (2006) reviews coffeehouses of the Enlightenment era and mentions some of the landmark work conceived and written in coffeehouses, including *Wealth of Nations* by Adam Smith, *Principia* by Isaac Newton, *Lettres philosophique* by François-Marie Voltaire, *Encyclopédie* by Denis Diderot, and *The Social Contract* by Jean-Jacques Rousseau. Thinkers then met, discussed, and even lectured in coffeehouses. Some had their mail delivered to coffeehouses. Some major business endeavors have started in coffeehouses, including Lloyds of London, the insurance giant. Even though the role of in-person contact has diminished in today's society, compared with the Enlightenment era, it is nevertheless reasonable to expect that this may need to change in the near future owing to the necessary industrial de-growth and down-scaling in regional economies, as projected by many authors mentioned in Chapter 2.

The gathering places discussed in Chapter 7 are the best candidates for creating and sustaining third places in the adaptation village, especially at block, quadrant, and village scales. Diversifying the casual as well as planned activities in these gathering places needs to be an important objective for the block, quadrant, and village administrations. When it comes to managing and regulating land uses, there is a close relationship between the concepts of loose space and third place; a dynamic regulation culture is essential not only for encouraging spontaneous activities and conviviality but also for sustaining meaningful social contact. When casual social contact coexists with an administrative forum in a gathering place, and when some creative business initiatives are also discussed and established in this place, the perfect stimulus is created for a successful third place that offers the above-mentioned social benefits. This needs to be a part of the vision for the social order in the adaptation village.

For further exploration of the concept, please see Oldenburg (1999), Oldenburg (Ed.) (2002), and Standage (2006).

Transition

Transition is an initiative aiming at creating resilient communities by means of localization. It refers to the "transition" that needs to happen from environmentally destructive and wasteful global economies to the network of resilient and self-sufficient lean economies that maximize the creative, social, and productive powers of residents at local scales. In terms of its commitment to land husbandry and sustainability, it shares philosophical underpinnings with permaculture. The term also refers to transition towns and Transition Network, a charity founded in 2007 with the objective of spreading the initiative by means of shared strategies. As of the writing of this book, 1130 transition initiatives (towns, districts, boroughs, valleys, peninsulas, islands, postal codes, and other community groups) are registered with Transition Network.

Rob Hopkins (2008), one of the founders of Transition Network, suggests that the transition concept is based on the following four assumptions:

1. That life with dramatically lower energy consumption is inevitable, and that it's better to plan for it than to be taken by surprise.
2. That our settlements and communities presently lack the resilience to enable them to weather the severe energy shocks that will company peak oil.
3. That we have to act collectively, and we have to act now.
4. That by unleashing the collective genius of those around us to creatively and proactively design our energy descent, we can build ways of living that are more connected, more enriching and that recognize the biological limits of our planet.

(p. 134)

One of the most telling examples of localization initiatives Hopkins (2008) discusses in his book is Britain's national "powerdown" policies that were implemented during World War II. Along with food rationing policies, the government implemented programs to initiate and support diverse home food production using modest means. In the 5 years following the beginning of the war, Britain reduced its food dependency almost 50 percent and created pockets of self-sufficiencies in various parts of the nation. More importantly, even though mechanized monoculture agriculture continued to provide carbohydrates and fats, it was the backyard gardens that produced most of the fresh fruit and vegetables that sustained healthy lives for many.

Many of the guiding principles of the transition movement are very much in line with the overarching objective "equilibrium in localization" and related principles discussed in this book. Seeing our neighbors as assets, investing in the creative potential of local networks and governance, and increasing the diversity of synergistic endeavors at household and neighborhood scales are among them.

We see a unique opportunity in establishing a strong relationship between permaculture, transition towns, and adaptive urbanism. The transition initiative has been successful in creating awareness about localization as an adaptation strategy. However, we need stronger steps in reshaping our urbanization patterns. We see proactive relocation (which can be initiated, enabled, and strengthened by the federal and state policies discussed in Chapter 4) as a unique opportunity to create a network of lean economies and self-sufficiencies. The adaptation village model provides a good guideline. The kind of urbanism that is structured by means of the balanced localization principles provided in this book will be able to empower a community to achieve the self-reliance that will be very much needed to cope with the realities of the climate crisis, an objective that is shared with Transition Network.

For further exploration of the term, please see Transition Network (transitionnetwork.org) and Transition US (transitionus.org). Also see the Transition US newsletter at www.transitionus.org/newsletter-archive/

BIBLIOGRAPHY

AghaKouchak, A., F. Chiang, L. S. Huning, C. A. Love, I. Mallakpour, O. Mazdiyasni, H. Moftakhari, S. M. Papalexiou, E. Ragno, and M. Sadegh. (2020). Climate extremes and compound hazards in a warming world. *Annual Review of Earth and Planetary Sciences*, vol. 48, pp. 20.1–20.30.

Alonso, B., and C. Guichon. (2020). *Human permaculture: Life design for resilient living*. New Society.

Asch, S. (1951). Effects of group pressure upon the modification and distortion of judgments. In H. Guetzkow (Ed.), *Groups, leadership and men: Research in human relations*. Carnegie Press, pp. 222–236.

Auerswald, P. E. (2015). Enabling entrepreneurial ecosystems: Insights from ecology to inform effective entrepreneurship policy. Kauffman Foundation Research Series on City, Metro, and Regional Entrepreneurship. Retrievable from https://papers.ssrn.com/sol3/papers.cfm?abstract_id=2673843

Baker, S. (2021). *Revolutionary power: An activist's guide to energy transition*. Island Press.

Baras, T. (2018). *DIY Hydroponic gardens: How to design and build an inexpensive system for growing plants in water*. Cool Springs Press.

Bernstein, S. (2011). *Aquaponic gardening: A step-by-step guide to raising vegetables and fish together*. New Society.

Berry, W. (2009). *Bringing it to the table: On farming and food*. Counterpoint Berkeley.

Bhatti H. J., and M Danilovic. (2018). Making the world more sustainable: Enabling localized energy generation and distribution on decentralized smart grid systems. *World Journal of Engineering and Technology*, no. 6, pp. 350–382.

Brueckner, J. (2014). Eliminate the mortgage interest deduction or tax imputed rent? Leveling the real-estate playing field. *Cityscape*, vol. 16, no. 1, pp. 215–218.

Chambers, Erve. (2000). *Native tours: The anthropology of travel and tourism*. Waveland Press.

Cisneros, G. H. (1995). *Defensible space: Deterring crime and building community*. U.S. Department of Housing and Urban Development.

Clark, S., and W. Teachout. (2012). *Slow democracy: Rediscovering community, bringing decision making back home*. Chelsea Green.

Crowe, T., and L. Fennelly. (2012). *Crime prevention through environmental design*. Butterworth-Heinemann.

164

Cummins, R. (2020). *Grassroots rising: A call to action on climate, farming, food, and a green new deal*. Chelsea Green.

Din, A. (2018). Intersecting opportunity zones with vacant business addresses. *Cityscape*, vol. 20, no. 3, pp. 277–280.

DiPasquale, D. (2011). Rental housing: Current conditions and the role of the federal policy. *Cityscape*, vol. 13, no. 2, pp. 57–70.

Dramstad, W. E., J. D. Olson, and T. T. T. Forman. (1996). *Landscape ecology principle in landscape architecture and land use planning*. Harvard University Graduate School of Design, Island Press, American Society of Landscape Architects.

Dovey, K., and K. Polakit. (2007). Urban spillage: Smooth and striated streetscapes in Bangkok. In K. A. Frank and Q. Stevens (Eds.), *Loose space: Possibility and diversity in urban life*. London, New York: Routledge, pp. 113–131.

Duany, A. (2011). *Theory and practice of agrarian urbanism*. The Prince's Foundation for the Built Environment.

Duany, A., and Brain, D. (2005). Regulating as if humans matter: The transect and post suburban planning. In E. Ben-Joseph and T. S. Szolg (Eds.), *Regulating place: Standards and the shaping of urban America*. Routledge, pp. 293–332.

Duany, A., and B. Falk (Eds.). (2020). *Transect urbanism: Readings in human ecology*. Center for Applied Transect Studies.

Duany, A., and R. Steuteville. (2021). Defining the 15-minute city. *Public Square: A CNU Journal*, Feb. 8. Retrievable at www.cnu.org/publicsquare/2021/02/08/defining-15-minute-city

Evans, M. A. (2015). Flushing the toilet has never been riskier. *The Atlantic*. Retrievable from www.theatlantic.com/technology/archive/2015/09/americas-sewage-crisis-public-health/405541/

FAO, IFAD, UNICEF, WFP, and WHO. (2019). *The state of food security and nutrition in the world 2019: Safeguarding against economic slowdowns and downturns*. Rome, FAO. Retrievable from www.fao.org/3/ca5162en/ca5162en.pdf

Fathy, H. (1986). *Natural energy and vernacular architecture: Principles and examples with reference to hot arid climates*. University of Chicago Press.

Fernando, A. N. (2007). Open-ended space In K. A. Frank and Q. Stevens (Eds.), *Loose space: Possibility and diversity in urban life*. London, New York: Routledge, pp. 54–72.

Fleming, D. (2016a). *Lean logic: A dictionary for the future and how to survive it*. Chelsea Green.

Fleming, D. (2016b). *Surviving the future: Culture, carnival and capital in the aftermath of the market economy*. Chelsea Green.

Franck, K. A., and Q. Stevens. (2007). Tying down loose space. In K. A. Frank and Q. Stevens (Eds.), *Loose space: Possibility and diversity in urban life*. Routledge, pp. 1–33.

Friedman, A. (2014). *Planning small and mid-sized towns: Designing and retrofitting for sustainability*. Routledge.

Gaul, M. G. (2019). *The geography of risk: Epic storms, rising seas, and the cost of America's coasts*. Sarah Crichton Books, Farrar, Straus & Giroux.

Givoni, B. (1998). *Climate considerations in building and urban design*. John Wiley.

Global Commission on Adaptation. (2020). *Adapt now: A global call for leadership on climate resilience*. Global Commission on Adaptation and World Resources Institute.

Gray, E., and NASA's Earth Science News Team. (2018). Unexpected future boost of methane possible from Arctic permafrost. NASA Global Climate Change: Vital Signs of the Planet. Retrievable at https://climate.nasa.gov/news /2785/unexpected-future-boost-of-methane-possible-from-arctic-permafrost/

Hakim, S. B. (1988). *Arabic-Islamic cities: Building and planning principles*. Kegan Paul.

Hindlian, A., S. Lawson, S. Banerjee, D. Duggan, and M. Hinds. (2019). *Taking the heat: Making cities resilient to climate change*. Global Markets Institute of the Goldman Sachs Group.

Holmgren, D. (2018). *Retro suburbia: The downshifter's guide to a resilient future.* Melliodora.

Hopkins, R. (2008). *The transition handbook: From oil dependency to local resilience.* Green Books.

IPCC. (2018). Summary for policymakers. In V. Masson-Delmotte, P. Zhai, H.-O. Pörtner, D. Roberts, J. Skea, P. R. Shukla, A. Pirani, W. Moufouma-Okia, C. Péan, R. Pidcock, S. Connors, J. B. R. Matthews, Y. Chen, X. Zhou, M. I. Gomis, E. Lonnoy, T. Maycock, M. Tignor, and T. Waterfield (Eds.), *Global warming of 1.5°C.* Retrievable from www.ipcc.ch/site/assets/uploads/sites/2/2019/05/SR15_SPM_version_report_LR.pdf

IPCC. (2020). Summary for policymakers. In P. R. Shukla, J. Skea, E. Calvo Buendia, V. Masson-Delmotte, H.-O. Pörtner, D. C. Roberts, P. Zhai, R. Slade, S. Connors, R. van Diemen, M. Ferrat, E. Haughey, S. Luz, S. Neogi, M. Pathak, J. Petzold, J. Portugal Pereira, P. Vyas, E. Huntley, K. Kissick, M. Belkacemi, and J. Malley (Eds.), *Climate Change and Land.* Retrievable from www.ipcc.ch/site/assets/uploads/sites/4/2020/02/SPM_Updated-Jan20.pdf

IPCC. (2021). Summary for Policymakers. In Masson-Delmotte, V., P. Zhai, A. Pirani, S. L. Connors, C. Péan, S. Berger, N. Caud, Y. Chen, L. Goldfarb, M. I. Gomis, M. Huang, K. Leitzell, E. Lonnoy, J.B.R. Matthews, T. K. Maycock, T. Waterfield, O. Yelekçi, R. Yu and B. Zhou (Eds.), *Climate change 2021: The physical science basis. Contribution of Working Group I to the Sixth Assessment Report of the Intergovernmental Panel on Climate Change.* Cambridge University Press. In Press. Retrievable from www.ipcc.ch/report/ar6/wg1/#SPM

Jacobs, J. (1961). *The death and life of great American cities.* Vintage Books.

Jacobs, J. (1984). *Cities and the wealth of nations: Principles of economic life.* Vintage Books.

Jenkins, J. (2005). *The humanure handbook: A guide to composting human manure.* Chelsea Green.

Klein, N. (2007). *Shock doctrine: The rise of disaster capitalism.* Random House.

Klein, N. (2019). *On: The (burning) case of a green new deal.* Simon & Schuster.

Knox, P. L., and H. Mayer. (2013). *Small town sustainability: Economic, social, and environmental innovation.* Birkhauser.

Knudsen, B. T., and A. M. Waade (Eds.). (2010). *Re-investing authenticity: Tourism, place and emotions.* Channel View.

Konya, A., and M. Vandenberg. (2011). *Design primer for hot climates.* Archimedia Press.

Lengen, J. V. (2008). *The barefoot architect: A handbook for green building.* Shelter.

Levine, L. (2014). Use less water … pollute less water: Sacramento can reduce sewage overflows through water conservation. Natural Resources Defense Council. Retrievable from www.nrdc.org/experts/larry-levine/use-less-waterpollute-less-water-sacramento-can-reduce-sewage-overflows-through

Loukaitou-Sideris, A., and R. Ehrenfeucht. (2012). *Sidewalks: Conflict and negotiation over public space.* MIT Press.

Lovelock, J. (2014). *A rough ride to the future.* Allen Lane (an imprint of Penguin Books).

Ludwig, Y., and K. Gimnig. (2021). *The cooperative culture handbook.* Foundation of Intentional Community (FIC) Publication.

Markham, B. (2012). *Maximizing your mini farm: Self-sufficiency in ¼ acre.* Skyhorse.

McCamant, K., and C. Durrett. (2011). *Creating cohousing: Building sustainable communities.* New Society.

Millstone, E., and T. Lang. (2008). *The atlas of food: Who eats what, where, and why.* University of California Press.

Mollison, B. (1988). *Permaculture: A designer's manual.* Tagari.

Mollison, B., and D. Holmgren. (1978). *Permaculture one: A perennial agriculture for human settlements.* Transworld.

Moltz, J. B., and B. McCray. (2012). *Small town rules: How big brands and small businesses can prosper in a connected economy.* Que Press.

Montgomery, C. (2013). *Happy city: Transforming our lives through urban design.* Farrar, Straus, & Giroux.

Nelson, A. C. (2013). *Reshaping metropolitan America: Development trends and opportunities to 2030.* Island Press.

Nelson, A. C. (2020). Chapter 2: Demographic changes and growing preference for missing middle housing. In D. Parolek and A. C. Nelson, *Missing middle housing: Thinking big and building small to respond to today's housing crisis.* Island Press, pp. 31–69.

Newman, O. (1972). *Defensible space: Crime prevention through urban design.* Macmillan.

Newman, P., T Beatley, and H. Boyer. (2017). *Resilient cities: Overcoming fossil fuel dependence.* Island Press.

Nikeghbali, S. (2017). Adapting design principles of traditional courtyard housing for future urban design. *Journal of Sustainable Development*, vol. 10, no. 6, pp. 200–213.

O'Connell, M. (2020). *Notes from an apocalypse: A personal journey to the end of the world and back.* Doubleday.

O'Connor, C., and J. O. Weatherall. (2019). *The misinformation age: How false beliefs spread.* Yale University Press.

Office of Community Oriented Policing Services (COPS), U. S. Department of Justice. (2012). *Using crime prevention through environmental design in problem solving.* A BiblioGov Publication.

Oldenburg, R. (1999). *The great good place: Cafés, coffee shops, bookstores, bars, hair salons and other hangouts at the heart of a community.* Marlowe.

Oldenburg, R. (Ed.) (2002). *Celebrating the third place: Inspiring stories about the "Great good places" at the heart of our communities.* Da Capo Press.

Onaran, K. (2019). *Crafting form-based codes: Resilient design, policy, and regulation.* Routledge.

Oreskes, N., and E. M. Conway. (2010). *Merchants of doubt: How a handful of scientists obscured the truth on issues of tobacco smoke and global warming.* Bloomsbury.

Parkins, W., and G. Craig. (2006). *Slow living.* Berg.

Parolek, D., and A. C. Nelson. (2020). *Missing middle housing: Thinking big and building small to respond to today's housing crisis.* Island Press.

Pearson C., S. Pilgrim, and J. Pretty (Eds.). (2010). *Urban agriculture: Diverse activities and benefits for city society. International Journal of Agricultural Sustainability.* Earthscan.

Petrini, C. (2005). *Slow food nation: Why our food should be good, clean, and fair.* Rizzoli.

Petrini, C. (2009). *Terra Madre: Forging a new global network of sustainable food communities.* Chelsea Green.

Petrini, C. (2013). *Food & freedom: How the slow food movement is changing the world through gastronomy.* Rizzoli ex libris.

Pollan, M. (2009). *In defense of food: An eater's manifesto.* Penguin.

Polyzoides, S., R. Sherwood, and J. Tice. (1992). *Courtyard housing in Los Angeles.* Princeton Architectural Press.

Ranganathan, J., R. Waite, T. Searchinger, and C. Hanson. (2018). How to sustainably feed 10 billion people by 2050, in 21 charts. World Resources Institute. Retrievable from www.wri.org/blog/2018/12/how-sustainably-feed-10-billion-people-2050-21-charts

Richter, B. (2014). *Beyond smoke and mirrors: Climate change and energy in the 21st century.* Cambridge University Press.

Rifkin, J. (2019). *The green new deal: Why the fossil fuel civilization will collapse by 2028, and the bold economic plan to save life on Earth.* St. Martin Press.

Sack, D. R. (1986). *Human territoriality: Its theory and history.* Cambridge University Press.

Scherer, T. F. (2015). *Individual home sewage treatment systems.* North Dakota State University Extension Service Report.

Schlosser, E. (2002). *The fastfood nation: The dark side of the all-American meal.* Perennial, Harper Collins.

Schwartz, H. L., R. W. Bostic, R. K. Green, V. J. Reina, L. M. Davis, and C. H. Augustine. (2016). *Preservation of affordable rental housing: Evaluation of the MacArthur Foundation's Window of Opportunity Initiative*. RAND Corporation.

ScottHanson, K., and C. ScottHanson. (2004). *The cohousing handbook: Building a place for community*. New Society.

Smil, V. (2019). *Growth: From microorganisms to megacities*. MIT Press.

Smith, J. A., and W. Winters. (2020). How to form a pandemic pod. *Greater Good Magazine: Science-Based Insights for a Meaningful Life* (July 17). Retrievable from: https://greatergood.berkeley.edu/article/item/how_to_form_a_pandemic_pod

Spencer, E. (2019). Plankton: Small organisms with a big role in the ocean. Ocean Conservancy. Blog retrievable at https://oceanconservancy.org/blog/2019/08/09/plankton-small-organism-big-role/

Srinivasan, R. (2017). *Whose global village? Rethinking how technology shapes our world*. New York University Press.

Srinivasan, R. (2019). *Beyond the valley: How innovators around the world are overcoming inequality and creating the technologies of tomorrow*. MIT Press.

Standage, T. (2006). *A history of the world in 6 glasses*. Walker, Bloomsbury.

Sterrett, D., and T. W. Smith. (2020). COVID response tracking study. NORC at the University of Chicago. Retrievable from: www.norc.org/Research/Projects/Pages/covid-response-tracking-study.aspx

Tasch, W. (2008). *Slow money: Investing as if food, farms, and fertility mattered*. Chelsea Green.

Thomas, P., S. Chaney, and C. Cutter. (2020). New Covid-19 layoffs make job reductions permanent. *The Wall Street Journal*, August 28. Retrievable from: www.wsj.com/articles/new-covid-19-layoffs-make-job-reductions-permanent-11598654257

Tinker, I. (1997). *Street foods: Urban food and employment in developing countries*. Oxford University Press.

United Nations Human Rights Council. (2019). Climate change and poverty. Report of the Special Rapporteur on extreme poverty and human rights. Retrievable at https://undocs.org/A/HRC/41/39

United States Global Change Research Program. (2018). *The climate report: The national climate assessment – impacts, risks, action in the United States*. Melville House.

United States, Department of Energy. (2009). Smart grid system report. Retrievable at www.energy.gov/sites/prod/files/2009%20Smart%20Grid%20System%20Report.pdf

Varoufakis, Y. (2017). *Talking to my daughter about the economy or, how capitalism works – and how it fails*. Farrar, Straus, & Giroux.

Vellinga, M., P. Oliver, and A. Bridge. (2007). *Atlas of vernacular architecture of the world*. Routledge.

Volk, J. (2017). *Compact farms: 15 proven plans for market farms on 5 acres or less*. Storey.

Walker, J. (2018). Co-op start-ups: Five tech firms run by their workers. NS Business. Retrievable from www.ns-businesshub.com/business/co-op-start-ups-tech-firms-run-by-workers/

Wallace-Wells, D. (2019). *The uninhabitable Earth: Life after warming*. Tim Duggan.

Wang, N. (1999). Rethinking authenticity in tourism experience. *Annals of Tourism Research*, vol. 26, no. 2, pp. 349–370.

Weber, K. (ed.). (2009). *Food Inc.: A participant guide: How industrial food is making us sicker, fatter, and poorer – and what you can do about it*. A Participant Media Publication. Perseus Book Group.

Weber, M. (1991). *The Protestant ethic and spirit of capitalism* (21st edition). Harper Collins Academic (original work published 1905).

Whitefield, P. (1993). *Permaculture in a nutshell*. Green Books.

Yeoman, K. B. (1993). *Water for every farm: Yeomans Keyline Plan*. Keyline Designs.

Yeomans, P. A. (1981). *Water for every farm: Using the Keyline Plan*. Second Back Row Press.

Note: **Bold** page numbers refer to tables; *italic* page numbers refer to figures and page numbers followed by "n" denote endnotes.